3/99

3000 800046 45260
St. Louis Community College

WITHDRAWN

D0206229

 St. Louis Community College

Forest Park
Florissant Valley
Meramec

Instructional Resources
St. Louis, Missouri

St. Louis Community College
at Meramec
Library

PRESENTING

Young Adult Horror Fiction

TUSAS 595

Twayne's United States Authors Series
Young Adult Authors

Patricia J. Campbell, General Editor

The Young Adult Authors books seek to meet the
need for critical studies of fiction for young adults.
Each volume examines the life and work of one
author, helping both teachers and readers of young
adult literature to understand better the writers they
have read with such pleasure and fascination.

PRESENTING

Young Adult Horror Fiction

Cosette Kies

TWAYNE PUBLISHERS
An Imprint of Simon & Schuster Macmillan
NEW YORK

Prentice Hall International
LONDON · MEXICO CITY · NEW DELHI · SINGAPORE · SYDNEY · TORONTO

Presenting Young Adult Horror Fiction
Cosette Kies

Copyright © 1992 by Twayne Publishers
All rights reserved. No part of this book may be reproduced or
transmitted in any form or by any means, electronic or mechanical,
including photocopying, recording, or by any information storage and
retrieval system, without permission in writing from the Publisher.

TWAYNE PUBLISHERS
An Imprint of Simon & Schuster Macmillan
1633 Broadway
New York, NY 10019-6785

Library of Congress Cataloging-in-Publication Data

Kies, Cosette N., 1936–
    Presenting young adult horror fiction / Cosette Kies.
        p.   cm. — (Twayne's United States authors series ; TUSAS
595. Young adult authors)
    Includes bibliographical references and index.
    ISBN 0-8057-8215-X
    1. Horror tales, American — History and criticism. 2. American
fiction — 20th century — History and criticism. 3. Young adults —
Books and reading. I. Title. II. Series: Twayne's United States
authors series ; TUSAS 595. III. Series: Twayne's United States
authors series. Young adult authors.
PS374.H67K54   1992
813'.087209—dc20   91-27002
                                                                        CIP

The paper used in this publication meets the minimum requirements
of American National Standard for Information Sciences—Permanence
of Paper for Printed Library Materials, ANSI Z39.48-1984. ∞™

Printed in the United States of America.

10 9 8 7 6 5 4

Contents

Preface

The nature of horror is elusive to pin down, as is the appeal of horror literature for those who enjoy it. Teenagers are some of the most enthusiastic fans of this genre. Certain writers, such as V. C. Andrews and Stephen King, are voted the favorite authors of teen readers time and time again. The popularity of horror literature with young adults can be neither denied nor ignored.

Presenting Young Adult Horror Fiction discusses some of the literature and American authors of horror that teenagers read. I have tried to show the development of horror literature within its historical context, as well as to demonstrate different ways of looking at these authors and their writings. I have included various elements of horror literature today, such as the traditional Gothic, satanism, true crime, splatterpunk, and dark fantasy.

The primary audience for this book is teenagers who are curious about life and authors and who like to read horror literature. Secondary audiences for the book are the adults in their lives: teachers, librarians, and parents who wonder at young adult interests and seek to understand young people better.

This book is structured differently from others in the Twayne Young Adult Authors series. The entire genre with only selected authors is covered, rather than highlighting a single author. Many fine writers have been excluded, not because of any lack on their part but because of my inability to fit in as many as I would have liked. My apologies to them.

Also, my apologies in advance for any incorrect or misinterpreted information about the authors. Time and distance did not permit personal contact with them to verify information already in print.

Thanks are owed many people, foremost among them my colleagues and students at Northern Illinois University who have shown interest and encouragement regarding the progress of this work. Particular thanks go to Beverly Balster, who helped with production; Marilynn Green, Andrea Banicki, and Tom Bell, who valiantly searched out tedious bibliographic details; and the reference staff of the Portsmouth (Virginia) Public Library, who did their best to find the carefully protected secret of V. C. Andrews's birth date. Thanks also go to my editors.

Horror literature is currently at its peak of popularity. Today more writers are working in the genre of horror fiction than ever before. As with any popular literary genre, not all the results are wonderful, yet the field is rich with thoughtful, provocative, and exciting books for people of many ages and tastes to enjoy as they choose.

Brief Chronology of Significant Horror Fiction

1765   Horace Wapole's *The Castle of Otranto.*

1794   Ann Radcliffe's *The Mysteries of Udolpho.*

1818   Mary Shelley's *Frankenstein; or, The Modern Prometheus.*

1840s   Edgar Allan Poe's short stories published in America.

1847   Emily Brontë's *Wuthering Heights.*

1872   Sheridan LeFanu's novella, "Carmilla."

1886   Robert Louis Stevenson's *The Strange Case of Dr. Jekyll and Mr. Hyde.*

1896   H. G. Wells's *The Island of Dr. Moreau.*

1897   Bram Stoker's *Dracula.*

1898   Henry James's *The Turn of the Screw.*

1930s   H. P. Lovecraft's stories.

1959   Shirley Jackson's *The Haunting of Hill House;* Robert Bloch's *Psycho.*

1967   Ira Levin's *Rosemary's Baby.*

1971   William Peter Blatty's *The Exorcist.*

1973   Stephen King's *Carrie.*

1976   Anne Rice's *Interview with the Vampire.*

1979   V. C. Andrews's *Flowers in the Attic*.

1984   The birth of splatterpunk.

1988   More horror books published in a single year than ever before.

1. The OK Factor in Horror

Many regard horror literature as not being "true literature" at all. True literature is serious, often written with a message or moral. Pure pleasure reading is somewhat suspect, since it is done primarily for enjoyment. As a result, many kinds of pleasure reading—genre fiction like mysteries, westerns, romances, and science fiction—are thought to be fluff. Certainly, the reasoning goes, such works cannot be deemed serious, true literature.

Most critics and others in the book world consider the worst of the genre pleasure books to be those written with the theme of horror. Parents, teachers, and librarians tend to feel nervous when they see teens reading horror books and attending the latest splatter film featuring blood and gore. What is the purpose of this? Where is the enjoyment in all this? they wonder. What kind of person really gets pleasure from all this awfulness? How can anyone find horror a theme for inspiring good feelings? What could possibly be good, or OK, about horror?

As lovers of horror know, the answer is easy. Horror scares us, and the relief following the realization that the horror is not real brings pleasure. Horror is fun just because it is scary and shocking. Not only does it scare and shock those of us who read horror, but it has the added value of scaring and shocking those who wonder how anyone could read the stuff in the first place. It is especially fun, of course, to shock those in authority, such as parents, teachers, and librarians.

Horror literature has been around awhile. It is considered to have had its beginnings with Gothic literature in the eighteenth century. Early Gothic literature, full of spookiness, lurid romances, supernatural happenings, and dramatic style, is also regarded as the parent of science fiction and certain types of romance novels. Any literary movement giving birth to three kinds of genre fiction is bound to be viewed as suspect by the gurus of serious literature. Obviously, however, even though Gothic literature was deplored in its own time, it was popular reading. The genre fiction it inspired is still read today.

The modern age of successful horror novels probably started in the late 1960s with the publication of Ira Levin's *Rosemary's Baby.* When it was followed soon after by William Peter Blatty's *The Exorcist,* a number of writers turned to the horror genre, with some crossovers from the then-still-popular Gothic romances, as well as mysteries and science fiction. About 10 years later the modern publishing phenomenon of Stephen King hit the bestseller lists, causing another surge upward in horror publishing and reading.

Yet some considered it an impermanent part of reading interest—or hoped it was. In the early 1980s such observers of the publishing scene as Judith Appelbaum commented about horror books, "Sales of horror and occult titles are down at B. Dalton and Waldenbooks, America's largest bookstore chains, and nearly 40% of the booksellers who took part in a recent *Book Review* survey report that titles in that category aren't selling as well as they did a year ago."[1] One can almost sense a note of hope and relief in this statement, for reviewers of the *New York Times* have never been noted for appreciating horror fiction. That hoped-for decline (or demise) of horror fiction in 1983 didn't happen, and the genre is still popular.

According to *Scream Factory* magazine, 182 horror novels/anthologies were published in 1988, an increase of 90% over 1987. This number does not include the also-high number of reissued titles.[2] Horror literature is still a favorite with many readers.

To illustrate just how popular horror fiction is with teens, a recent poll of young adult readers in the Cleveland suburbs resulted in a list of 10 favorite books, 4 of which are horror stories: *Pet Sematary,* by Stephen King; *Flowers in the Attic,* by V. C. Andrews; *It,* by Stephen King; and *Chain Letter,* by Christopher Pike.[3]

As with any popular fiction, critics are forced to pay more attention to such works than they may wish to, and when authors like Stephen King continually make the best-seller lists and become rich, critics must consider what has happened. After deploring the lowness of popular taste, the critics must look for something to explain it all. What is there about horror literature that makes so many people want to buy and read it? It's easier to find possible explanations, such as the escape factor, in other kinds of popular-genre books, but horror enters into the dark realm of fear. A lot of adults don't like to be scared, for they find the real world scary enough. As a result, some critics apparently feel that those who do like horror fiction haven't grown up and that horror fiction is a sort of immature fiction for immature readers. The persistence of horror as a form of literature, however, shows that its readers are loyal to their genre, and many of them don't care what the critics think.

Creating a mood of fear is vital to creating horror books people want to read. Graham Masterton, a noted British writer now spending much time in the United States, says, "Fear is the prime ingredient of all successful horror novels, although naturally you have to fulfill the terrible threat with which you have presented your characters. You can't write about vampires who never get around to sinking their fangs into anybody, or werewolves who don't tear anybody's lungs out, or zombies who stay in their coffins and don't shuffle around shopping malls dropping bits of themselves wherever they go."[4] Masterton, a successful writer of screenplays and the author of such popular horror works as *The Manitou, Tengu, The Mirror,* and *Dream Warriors,* continues, "But creating an atmosphere of fear is far more important (and far more difficult) than creating a moment of disgust. It is the atmosphere of brooding evil that will make your horror novel successful . . . the feeling that you implant inside your reader's reluctant mind that the terrible threat is hanging not only over your characters but over him, too" (Masterton, 15).

Even though some critics may concede that it takes writing skill to create an atmosphere of fear, there is still a tendency to criticize even the most popular horror writers and their readers. Henry Kisor, book editor of the *Chicago Sun-Times,* in writing about Stephen King's opus *The Dark Half,* says:

> Narrative, however, is the least of the literary virtues which also include style, wit, and economy of expression, none of which King seems to possess. . . . Speaking of obscenity, King's dialogue is contemptible. In the mouths of King's characters (heroes and heroines as well as bad guys) every four-letter word extant undergoes every possible permutation, none of them original. . . .
>
> The horror genre, almost by definition, rewards bloody-minded imagination more than it does cool skill. Having stumbled upon the right buttons to push, the clumsiest writer can win a following among the masses.[5]

Yet Stephen King has been praised by many for his storytelling ability and realistic depiction of everyday life. It is possible that some critics like to trash horror because doing so is easy: if you can't explain its popularity, then dump on the genre as a whole.

The image most people have of the readers of horror books is that of some sort of weird, teenage boy—at best a cheerful young Stephen King. Booksellers in 1983 volunteered the following capsule descriptions of buyers of horror fiction, however, showing that love of horror literature is not limited to any single, easily defined demographic group:

- Mostly middle class, older, in their late 40s and 50s—they buy only horror.
- Mostly men.
- Mostly fat ladies. (Appelbaum, 39)

Why does horror appeal to a such wide range of readers? It's hard to say, but obviously the writers and publishers of horror fiction are willing to produce this "awful" literature. The bottom line, at least for many publishers today, is not the reputation of the literature or even what the critics may say. It is sales that count in the end. As long as horror literature sells, it will be written and published.

For many buyers of horror fiction, there is a sense of shame, a pervasive societal attitude that *it*—horror literature—is unwholesome and may even be un-American somehow. Scholars who work in the area are often viewed askance by their colleagues and have problems getting their research and publications accepted as serious work. It just isn't "respectable" to take horror literature seriously.[6]

Why does horror appeal to teenagers? Fear and fun seem to be important factors in the popularity of horror literature, not only with teens but with many other people. A number of theories seem to back up this idea. One has been suggested by Harvard sociologist Daniel Bell: "In America, failure to have fun lowers one's self-esteem. Teen-agers, for whom self-esteem is a fragile thing, may read piquant romances and horror stories because the quick payoff makes them feel good about themselves. Formulaic fiction for young adults takes the endemic condition of teen-agers and exacerbates it with the promise of fun-filled, painless experience."[7]

Caryn James has another idea about why horror stories and films are popular with many people, including teens—they're like the continuing fantasies of soap operas. She says:

> Elm Street or Jason's summer resort town of Crystal Lake are truly other worlds, operating under laws peculiar to daytime serials. The only occupations seem to be doctor and police chief. Children change from babies to teen-agers between episodes: Jason and Freddy wipe out a whole generation each film, so they need fresh victims to grow fast. And something in the air or water causes collective amnesia. Just as soap opera characters can be acquitted of murder one day and elected to Congress the next, people stay in their haunted houses on Elm Street, oblivious to the community's high mortality rate for teen-agers.[8]

Robert Englund, the actor and now–cult hero who plays Freddy on Elm Street, suggests:

> It's not so much that people idolize Freddy, although there is a certain punk sensibility [in] liking Freddy, it's because he's an anarchist, out there trashing the white, Anglo-Saxon, middle class that inhabits Elm Street.
>
> Another factor in Freddy's popularity is audience anticipation. They love to watch Freddy manipulating his potential victims, using their fantasies and tragic flaws to abuse them. It's fun, like watching Ralph Kramden on "The Honeymooners," anticipating when he's going to yell at Alice.[9]

Teens are right—horror books and movies are fun if they're not taken too seriously. A list of teen best-sellers for September 1989 displayed at Waldenbooks shows the majority of titles are horror books or thrillers.

Waldenbooks Top 10 Young Adult Best-sellers for September 1989

1. *Fear Street—Surprise Party,* by R. L. Stine
2. *Chain Letter,* by Christopher Pike
3. *Fog,* by Caroline Cooney
4. *Tangled Web,* by L.M. Montgomery [an aberration]
5. *Slumber Party,* by R. L. Stine
6. *Babysitter,* by R. L. Stine
7. *Weekend,* by Christopher Pike
8. *Karate Kid #3,* by B. B. Hiller
9. *Scavenger Hunt,* by Christopher Pike
10. *Fear Street—The New Girl,* by R. L. Stine

Horror literature appeals to a broad range of ages, including adolescents: both young teens barely in high school and older teens in college. Two interesting research studies were reported in *Horrorstruck,* a periodical that, sadly, is now defunct but was devoted to the genre.

In the first study Elizabeth Massie, herself a published horror writer, discovered that her seventh-grade students in rural Virginia loved horror. In a spontaneous, round-robin writing exercise 74.9 percent of the class members wrote some aspect of horror into their stories. These are young teens who prefer reading Dean Koontz to books written for their age level. They'd rather watch *Friday the Thirteenth* on video than *The Black Stallion*.[10]

The writing exercise produced such stories as

- one about a mouse named Arnold Swartzenmouse, who eats cat brains and drinks gut milk shakes;
- another about a baby who is deformed with snakeskin and antennae; and
- conventional tales of ghosts, mass murders, and—most gross of all—a snot-sucking vampire (Massie, 13).

In a follow-up to the revelations of the writing exercise, Massie asked her students to respond to an open-ended questionnaire about why they liked horror books and movies. One girl wrote, "Scary stories are good because you don't know what's going to happen next. It keeps you really interested. You always know in the Sweet Valley books that the girl is going to get one of the boys for her boyfriend. That's why I like scary stories," (Massie, 14). Another respondent said, "*Flowers in the Attic* was good because the grandmother was terrible and you wanted to get revenge on her. I was hoping the kids would kill her." And as a counterbalance to those young people who seem to love the special effects in horror movies, one respondent said, "Reading scary stuff is better than watching it. My mom doesn't like me watching it anyway. But in books you can stop it when you want to." As to a general sense of why they like horror, the respondents said things like this: "Being scared is fun because it's exciting." "It's good and exciting. I get chillbumps and they feel good. You know?" "It's creepy and scary and I like it. And it doesn't last too long most of the time" (Massie, 14).

The other study reported in *Horrorstruck* was done by D. W. Taylor in a small nondenominational liberal arts college in Pennsylvania in a special class entitled "Contemporary Horror Fiction." This class was popular, difficult to get into, and full of enthusiastic aficionados of horror literature. Taylor decided to focus his study on some finer points of horror fiction. One aspect he investigated was what qualities the students viewed as essential to good horror stories. One element was the overwhelming winner—suspense. The second most important criterion was believable characters (important in all kinds of literature). A surprisingly high number of respondents disliked graphic gore, preferring more subtle, suggestive ways to make the shivers happen.[11]

Another aspect of Taylor's study dealt with what today's readers of horror fiction *don't* want. Interestingly enough, more than 80 percent condemned long drawn-out stories containing too much detail. A high number of students disliked predictability and found excessive violence, gore, and explicit sex disagreeable (Taylor, 14-16).

What, then, is the appeal of horror fiction? Despite much analysis of the literature and exploration into the psyches of those who like to read it, the true appeal of this genre remains elusive, but perhaps no more so than the appeal of any other type of popular literature; however, there does not seem to be so strong a motivation to find out *why* people read romances, westerns, and mysteries. These latter works are more respectable forms of literature, safer kinds of books. They are more closely aligned to what we believe the world to really be like, or what we would like it to be. It's OK for every girl to dream of finding a Prince Charming, for good guys to thwart rustlers and criminals. But where is the OK factor in horror? Even though many horror books end on a note of hope and good often prevails in some way, the evil that must be conquered is something many do not care to think about.

Perhaps part of our current interest and concern for horror literature and movies comes from the increasing real horrors of the world today. Geraldo Rivera tells us that heavy-metal music can inspire kids to become satanists and murderers. The world of drugs inspires horrible criminal activities. Terrorists perpetrate senseless crimes, and awful realities hit us daily on the news broadcasts.

Kids growing up today deserve fun that doesn't hurt anyone. For a lot of teens, horror literature provides that fun. Horror literature is the same as any other kind of literature—it can be great fun for those who like it, and those who don't like it can choose not to read it. In the end, it's all a matter of taste.

2. Horror and the Gothic Tradition: V. C. Andrews

As a literary genre, horror is usually said to have begun with Gothic literature in the eighteenth century, primarily in England. The generally accepted starting point is the publication of Horace Wapole's *The Castle of Otranto* in 1765, when the country that would become the United States of America was still a colony of Great Britain.

The Castle of Otranto had all the features that still define Gothic literature: spooky surroundings, moldering old castles, mysterious happenings, elements of the supernatural, and menaced young women. The novel became popular immediately and started a strain of writing that became firmly entrenched in Great Britian and the United States during the following decades and centuries. Moreover, in becoming a type of literature in its own right, Gothic literature became the basis, at least in part, for other types of fiction, including horror, science fiction, and mysteries.

Women were early lovers of Gothic literature, and they became Gothic writers as well. In nineteenth-century England such writers as Ann Radcliffe and the Brontë sisters wrote stories in the Gothic mold that were popular with many readers. Also during that century in England the ghost story as a distinct form of literature was evolving, and a number of writers, including M. R. James and Algernon Blackwood, devoted themselves to this genre. Stories of ghosts and haunted houses are still popular in many countries today. Favored ghost/haunted-house books in the United States have included *The Haunting of Hill House,* by Shirley Jackson; *Ghost Story,* by Peter Straub; and the supposedly true story of *The Amityville Horror,* reported by Jay Anson.

In the United States Edgar Allan Poe made his great contribution to horror literature by becoming the acknowledged founder of the American school of the macabre with his short stories of horror and mystery. Yet America still looked to England for leadership in cultural matters, including literature, and followers of the Gothic tradition and the ghost story abounded on both sides of the Atlantic. Many writers, even those who achieved fame for other types of writing, enjoyed penning occasional Gothic thrillers. One such writer was Louisa May Alcott—best known for her wholesome tales of family life, exemplified by *Little Women*—who published a number of ripsnorting, lurid Gothic stories.

Although Gothic literature was popular from its beginning, it was also ridiculed by many for its excesses. Jane Austen's *Northanger Abbey* slyly pokes fun at the Gothic tradition, as did many other authors and critics. But the public loved it, and it's easy to see why, as this passage from Ann Radcliffe's *The Mysteries of Udolpho,* first published in 1794, demonstrates: "While Emily gazed with awe upon the scene, footsteps were heard within the gates, and the undrawing of bolts; after which an ancient servant of the castle appeared, forcing back the huge folds of the portal to admit his lord. As the carriage-wheels rolled heavily under the portcullis, Emily's heart sank, and she seemed as if she was going into her prison; the gloomy court into which she passed, served to confirm the idea; and her imagination, ever awake to circumstance, suggested even more terrors than her reason could justify."[1]

Gothic literature, like many other types of literature, seems to go through cycles of greater and lesser popularity. Certain elements are stressed at different times, depending primarily on what the public wants to buy. Probably the last significant period of Gothic romance popularity in the United States was in the 1960s and 1970s with formulaic Gothic romances.

It is difficult to say with certainty when horror literature became a distinct form, and it cannot be said that Gothic literature and horror literature are mutually exclusive today. To be successful, a Gothic story of the twentieth century must have elements of horror, whether those elements be supernatural or psychological.

Gothic literature is still very much a part of mainstream American literature. During the past century a form of regional Gothic, the southern Gothic, evolved as a separate literary genre. Today one of the best-selling authors in the Gothic tradition is a Virginian named Virginia Cleo Andrews.

V. C. Andrews:
If Love Is So Strong, Can It Be Wrong?

The face of fear I display in my novels is not the pale specter from the sunken grave, nor is it the thing that goes bump in the night. Mine are the deep-seated fears established when we are children, and they never go away: the fear of being helpless, the fear of being trapped, the fear of being out of control.[2]
—V. C. Andrews

V. C. Andrews, known to her friends and family as Virginia, was born in the Tidewater region of Virginia. Her family had lived in that part of the country for generations and still lived in Virginia's grandfather's house in Portsmouth. Her family was apparently close, as is typical of many southern families. She was the only daughter of her parents, who also had two sons, Eugene and Bill.

Virginia's father was originally a career navy man, but Virginia's mother asked him to settle down. He did, becoming a tool-and-die maker. At one point the Andrews family moved to Rochester, New York, but returned to Portsmouth before Virginia finished high school. During her formal schooling days Virginia

Chronology: V. C. Andrews's Life and Works

1940–1962 Born Virginia Cleo Andrews on 6 June (1940–43?) in Portsmouth, Virginia, the daughter of Lillian Lilnora (Parker) and William Henry Andrews (a career navy man and later a tool-and-die maker). (The following events in Andrews's early years have been documented. Exact dates, however, are uncertain.) Family moves to Rochester, New York. Family returns to Virginia. At age 15, falls down stairs at school, triggering lifelong crippling arthritis. Graduates from Woodrow Wilson High School in Portsmouth. Completes four-year correspondence art program at home. Earns living as fashion illustrator and portrait painter.

1963 After father dies, moves with mother to Manchester, Missouri, a suburb of St. Louis; home of a brother. Moves with mother to Apache Junction, Arizona; home of other brother.

1972 Returns with mother to Portsmouth, Virginia. Sensational short story, "I Slept with My Uncle on My Wedding Night," is published by confession magazine during this period.

1979 First novel, *Flowers in the Attic,* published by Pocket Books.

1980 Sequel, *Petals on the Wind.*

1981 Sequel to *Flowers, If There Be Thorns.* Moves with mother to Virginia Beach, Virginia.

1982 Only book not in a series, *My Sweet Audrina,* published.

1984 Sequel to *Flowers, Seeds of Yesterday.*

1985 New series starts with *Heaven.*

1986 Sequel to *Heaven, Dark Angel.*

1986 Dies of cancer on 19 December.

1987– *Garden of Shadows* and other books published posthumously.

1988 Film of *Flowers in the Attic* released.

showed great artistic promise, a quality encouraged by her teachers. Virginia also loved to read and began making up her own stories at an early age. A note to readers from the publishers in the book *Dark Angel* includes the following statement written by her:

> I was brought up in a working-class environment, with a father who loved to read as much as I did. When I was seven he took me to the public library and signed me up for my first library card. He went home with two books. I went home with nine.
>
> Books opened doors I hadn't even realized were there. They took me up and out of myself, back into the past, forward into the future; put me on the moon, placed me in palaces, in jungles, everywhere. When finally I did reach London and Paris— I'd been there before.
>
> When books fail to give what I need, dreams supply the rest. A long time ago I dreamed I was rich and famous—and I saw flowers growing in the attic.
>
> Dreams can come true, no matter what fate chooses to place as obstacles to hurdle, crawl under, or go around. Somehow I always manage to reach the far side. To have a goal and achieve it despite everything is my only accomplishment. If I give a few million readers pleasure and escape along the way, I do the same for myself.[3]

V. C. Andrews reported her childhood as being a happy one and certainly not a model for the plots of her books. If anything, young Virginia felt her childhood was simply too uneventful, and she early began to make up stories about people who led far more exciting lives than she. There were evidently no unhealthy undercurrents in her family: Andrews's brothers were not her love/lust objects; nor did her parents mistreat her in any way—it is unlikely they locked her up in an attic for years, the fate of the Dollanganger children in Andrews's first successful novel. Her stories were the product of her own imagination, not retellings of personal wrongs being spilled out as a catharsis to heal a damaged psyche.

While still a teenager Andrews fell down the stairs at school, apparently twisting her back badly in the fall. Bone spurs formed on her spine, and crippling arthritis set in. Operations to alleviate the condition only made the situation worse; ultimately, she was sentenced to life as a partial cripple, using braces and wheel-chairs. This part of her life no doubt prompted her to place a num-ber of her characters in wheelchairs, although she did not use this aspect as an excuse to complain about her own handicapped con-dition. Rather, the people in her books learn to live with their limitations, probably mirroring Andrews's own attitude about her infirmity.

She was very secretive about her age, a behavior dating from an incident while she was still a teenager. She had made friends with people a few years younger than she who seemed disap-pointed to learn she was older. Thereafter she viewed age as an artificial determinant of a person and would never tell her age to anyone (Winter 1985, 164–65). Andrews said she finished high school, but with her father's death she needed to earn money. She studied art at home, eventually becoming a professional commer-cial artist and portrait painter. For a time she and her mother lived near her brothers and their families, first in the St. Louis, Missouri, area and then in Fort Apache, Arizona. Ten years later she and her mother returned to Portsmouth and settled down, with Andrews determined to start a new career as a successful author. She never lived in the beautiful Appalachian mountains, the setting frequently used in her books.

Her first published work was a sensational story, "I Slept with My Uncle on My Wedding Night," which appeared in a pulp confession magazine. Though such magazines do not pay authors well, the publication of her story must have given the struggling writer hope, as she continued to write at least 30 pages every night. Her agent and editors encouraged her as well, and she kept going. Finally, in the late 1970s, the manuscript of her long novel *The Obsessed* attracted more attention than she had previously received. She was urged to cut the story to a more manageable length and to "get more gutsy."

Getting more gutsy had been Andrews's instinct as well, and following the advice she had received, she drafted the final out-line of *Flowers in the Attic* in a single evening, including in the outline those elements which made her an instant best-selling

writer: psychological child abuse, murder, adultery, imprisonment, greed, passion, and incest. This first book, with a plot like
a ferocious fairy tale and written in a luridly romantic style, was
apparently what a lot of members of the book-buying public had
been waiting for eagerly. Andrews herself explained the immediate success of this and later books with the comment "because it
stirs up primal fears we all have in us that mama is going to turn
against us and leave us."[4]

There are conflicting explanations about the decision to publish
her books in the United States as written by "V. C. Andrews,"
rather than "Virginia Andrews." One version is that the publishers felt the first book would be more successful if the buying public thought a man had written it. In an interview with Douglas E.
Winter, Andrews claims the publishers had promised to use her
full first name, Virginia, and that the final use of "V. C." was a
printing error (Winter 1985, 175). Her books are published in
other countries with "Virginia Andrews" emblazoned on the cover.
She dedicated that first book to her mother, somewhat tongue-in-
cheek, one supposes, for her mother didn't really approve of the
themes in the book and later claimed never to have read any of
her daughter's novels.

After the smash success of her first publication, Andrews was
approached by *People* magazine for an interview. She was disap-
pointed with the results, which pictured her as an odd, reclusive
woman, older than she really was. This experience understandably made her leery of other interviewers, and besides a few that
appeared in local newspapers, the only good interview with V. C.
Andrews is one done by Douglas E. Winter for a book about modern horror writers, *Faces of Fear*.

Despite her physical disability and the report in *People* to the
contrary, Andrews enjoyed travel and elegant dinners in fashion-
able restaurants. She promoted her books as requested by her
publisher and generously gave talks to local groups in her hometown area. She obviously enjoyed her success and the accompanying attention. She was not a recluse; she was an author. By its
nature writing is a lonely job that requires solitude, but Andrews
was by no means a voluntary hermit.

New books by V. C. Andrews followed, with a new best-seller being published about once a year. She also worked on other books, including a fantasy trilogy drafted earlier for young adults, *The Gods of Green Mountain*; although she had hoped for publication of this trilogy, apparently the project was never finalized by her publisher. She also worked on a historical novel set in France, a book that to date has not been published. She was not satisfied with her published works being classified as horror literature, but critics generally agree that they fall into that category partly through elimination, since they don't fit any other kind of genre fiction. Horror is not inaccurate as a descriptor, for there is a horror of fascination and awfulness throughout V. C. Andrews's books, as well as the feeling of an inevitable fate.

Although her books were rarely well received by the critics, the public loved Andrews's stories, and she enjoyed new financial security. She and her mother moved from Portsmouth to neighboring Virginia Beach, where Andrews continued to write. She is reported to have had a mirror mounted over her typewriter (later a word processor) so that she could look at herself as she wrote. She claimed this practice assisted her by helping her to project better. When working on a book, she would write with great concentration and intensity, losing weight in her fixation on the project at hand.

Andrews did not include in her books information about the supernatural. She believed in ESP, however, and considered herself to be somewhat psychic. She had haunting, fleeting visions of earlier existences, pointing to her belief in reincarnation. She also believed she had prophetic dreams, and she took these quite seriously. She claimed she had had a dream in her youth in which she saw herself on crutches as an adult, foretelling her disability. Although reared as a Southern Baptist, she was obviously not a straitlaced practitioner in later life, perhaps believing that inner spirituality was more suited to her own beliefs (Winter 1985, 175).

Sadly enough, just when financial, if not critical, success would seem to have made her dreams come true, she was diagnosed as having cancer, and she died in late 1986. Her books, plotted in advance of her death, are still being published. All titles continue to sell very well.

What is V. C. Andrews's appeal to her readers? The answer is best summed up by Douglas Winter, who said:

> The best-known chronicler of childhood terrors is V. C. Andrews, the top-selling woman writer identified with the field of horror fiction; indeed, she has been called the "fastest-selling" writer of *any* kind of fiction in this decade—more than twenty million copies of her books have been in print since her first novel, *Flowers in the Attic,* appeared in 1979. Her books, a mingling of adult fairy tale and psychological terror, earn the label of "horror" more by default than design. . . . [Speaking of Dollanganger series]: it is animated by nightmarish passions of greed, cruelty, and incest, yet is told in romantic fairy tale tones, producing the most highly individualistic tales of terror of this generation.[5]

The Dollanganger Series

Flowers in the Attic

V. C. Andrews's first published book, *Flowers in the Attic* (1979), became an instant popular success. Pocket Books, her publisher, committed $100,000 for promotion, unusual for a first-time, unknown author of an original paperback. To gamble on an unknown like V. C. Andrews attests to the faith of her editor, Ann Patty, for the potential selling power of *Flowers.*

Flowers was probably culled from a longer manuscript, *The Obsessed.* Some of the unused material in *Flowers* may have been incorporated into later Dollanganger books, for the immediate success of *Flowers* prompted the continuing story of the dysfunctional Foxworth family through a total of five titles. Although *Flowers* was the first published, *Garden of Shadows,* the last published book in the series, is a prequel, describing what happened before *Flowers.* For those who have not read the series, it is best to read the books in the order of their publication, for the prequel might spoil the surprises as they are disclosed in the other four books. Moreover, the prequel, *Garden,* is Olivia's story, and for many readers it might be a pity to soften feelings toward the cruel grandmother of the Dollanganger siblings.

When published in November 1979 *Flowers* became a top seller not only because of the publisher's promotion budget, store displays, and general media hype. It was fast word-of-mouth promotion that truly made *Flowers* such an instant best-seller. This is the kind of "promotion" publishers seek, for it is the recommendation of a book by friends and relatives that encourages sales. For a book by an unknown author to achieve such fast best-selling status, the word-of-mouth promotion must have been excellent.

Flowers starts the story of the Dollanganger siblings. In the beginning Chris is 14, Cathy is 12, and the twins, Cory and Carrie, are 4. They live in Pennsylvania with their too-good-to-be-true parents. All the family members are beautiful, blond, and blue-eyed. Friends jokingly call them the Dresden Dolls, partly as a play on their unusual last name and partly for their handsome Nordic appearance.

Tragedy strikes, however, for their father, Christopher Dollanganger, is killed in a car accident on his way home for his thirty-sixth birthday party. Gloom and doom fall over the Dresden Dolls' home. Unlike a number of other stories, this is not a tale of dealing with parental death, however; this is a story that deals with darker, more horrific themes, problems that mount to seemingly impossible heights.

Because of money difficulties the children are told by their mother they must leave their comfortable home and possessions in order to seek help from her estranged parents. Sneaking away from their once-happy home with only four suitcases among them, the sorrowful band travels by train to the mountains of western Virginia. In the middle of the night the children and their mother get off at a dark, deserted station and walk miles to a forbidding mansion, Foxworth Hall. They are slipped into the house through the back door and taken silently to a grim room by an old woman whose first words to the mother concern the beauty of the children, but then is quickly followed by a question regarding any hidden abnormalities the children may possess.[6]

The old woman is the grandmother, and the children's mother, Corrine, must revert to a subservient role by following orders and doing penance for sin. The children are given strict orders not to leave the bedroom-bathroom suite. At first they believe this restriction is only for one night, until Corrine is able to make the necessary explanations to her father. But the one night becomes another and another. Finally the children realize they are imprisoned for an indefinite time, for their mother must wait for her father to die before she can inherit his great wealth, all for her own children's benefit. The children's prison is enlarged to include a huge attic, full of musty treasures, and the children become "flowers in the attic."

The story is told in the first person by Cathy, who becomes a surrogate mother to the twins, as Chris becomes a substitute father. The grandmother visits early each morning with a basket of food for the day, along with stern admonitions to never look on one another's nakedness. The reader discovers that Corrine and her husband had been related; Christopher was Corrine's half-uncle. The older Foxworths had disowned their only child, Corrine, when she entered into this sinful, forbidden, and incestuous relationship; Dollanganger was adopted as the younger family's name. The children would never have known any of this except for their father's death and their mother's desperate attempt to regain her parents' favor and fortune.

It is clear that the austere, religious grandmother is constantly seeking imperfections in her grandchildren as proof of their parents' sin in committing incest. She also fears that history will repeat itself, with Cathy and Chris becoming lovers. In the first part of the book Corrine is loving and caring with her children, visiting often and trying to put their fears to rest. At one point, when Cathy is worrying over all this, Corrine reacts: "Suddenly, she jerked up her head and looked at me. Did she see something doubting, something questioning? Her eyes shadowed, grew deep, dark. 'Join hands,' she ordered forcefully, bracing her shoulders, releasing one of Chris's hands. 'I want you to repeat after me: We are perfect children. Mentally, physically, emotionally, we are wholesome, and godly in every way possible. We have as much right to live, love, and enjoy life as any other children on this earth'" (*Flowers*, 104).

Living in such a strange, abnormal way, with no contact with others their own age, no school, and no real friends beyond themselves, the children become introspective and brooding. The role of artificial parenthood weighs heavily on Chris and Cathy. They see their mother distancing herself from them; not visiting as frequently and substituting expensive gifts for her time. The grandmother increasingly becomes their only predictable link with the real world, and the children can only fear and hate her.

They continue as best they can with their lives, looking ahead with hope to a time when they will at last be released from their confining quarters. Cathy studies ballet alone, teaching herself to go *en pointe*; Chris studies science and medical books; and they try to teach the twins some basic three Rs. Cathy dreams of a career as a dancer, and Chris is determined to be a doctor someday.

The four youngsters try to keep up their spirits, but there are continual setbacks. The grandfather, although ailing and in a wheelchair, seems to hang stubbornly to life, and Corrine admits to the children that she will never be able to tell him that children were born in her incestuous marriage. It is obvious their mother has rejoined her social set in the neighborhood. She now has a suitor, Bart Winslow, and the children learn after the fact that they have married. The twins become frail in their unhealthy environment, and Chris and Cathy are faced with puberty and growing emotions they cannot control.

The children learn that the grandfather has died, finally, but they must continue to stay in the attic, for a condition in his will states that if Corrine ever has children, past or future, she loses everything. Passion finally overwhelms Chris and Cathy, who consummate their love, though they give in only once. Cory sickens and dies, leaving the other children heartbroken. Chris and Cathy are desperate. They know they must escape, for they will never be able to count on their mother again, and they know Cory was deliberately poisoned. They have been in their prison for more than three years.

Chris, Cathy, and fragile Carrie escape from the terrible home of the Foxworths and set forth on their own, ready to face the real world. They take with them, however, memories that will remind and haunt them forever of their past. The Dollanganger saga has begun.

Petals on the Wind

Flowers, as noted, was a real hit with the reading public, especially teenage girls. Cathy's story appeals to many readers, for here is a girl with fantastic problems to face, problems of the kind usually found only in fairy tales. The critics, however, were not kind to the first book in the Dollanganger series, one reviewer going so far as to say, *"Flowers in the Attic* may well be the worst book I have ever read."[7] It is not known how Andrews reacted to such reviews. The financial success of the book must have helped soothe possible hurt feelings, but she did say once that her ultimate goal was to have her books considered classics of their time (Jordan, 2).

Negative reviews did not cause the publisher to pause in rushing the second book in the series, *Petals on the Wind,* to the bookstores less than a year later, in June 1980. The excellent sales of *Flowers* prompted the company to move the publishing date of *Petals* forward a few months, making it a perfect purchase for those looking for a good summertime read. *Petals* became a bestseller as quickly as *Flowers,* and *Flowers* returned to the bestseller lists briefly as new readers discovered the series.

V. C. Andrews now appears to be in high writing stride, for the melodrama that surrounds Cathy Foxworth is the stuff that makes for real page-turning sagas. Her writing style, although scorned by some critics, moves the plot along with a florid vocabulary and descriptions reminiscent of "Lifestyles of the Rich and Famous." Critics may term her characters cardboard and two-dimensional, but they are characters with exciting lives. Readers looking for relief from their own problems and boring lives find splendid escape in the continuing adventures of Chris, Cathy, and Carrie.

In *Petals* the young Dollangangers are miraculously befriended by Dr. Paul Sheffield, who convinces them that their plan to go to Sarasota, Florida, and join a circus is unrealistic. Dr. Paul, as the children call him, is a lonely widower who gains legal custody of the three with no problems. Cathy continues her dancing lessons; Chris studies to go to college; and Carrie goes to a special school. Yet problems arise, not the least of which are Cathy's feelings for Chris; her new stepfather, Bart Winslow; Dr. Paul; and Julian, the mercurial, handsome son of her dance teacher.

Chris is not so fickle, for at one point when Cathy is contemplating marriage with Dr. Paul, Chris cries:

> "Damn it, Cathy, I want you! You don't plan to have children anyway, so *why can't it be me?*"
>
> I'd drawn away when he released my shoulders. When his words stopped I ran to fling my arms around him as he clutched at me, as if I were the one and only woman who could save him from drowning. And we'd both drown if I did as he wanted. "Oh, Chris, what can I say? Momma and Daddy made their mistake in marrying each other—and we were the ones to pay the price. We can't risk repeating their mistake!"
>
> "Yes we can!" he fervently cried. "We don't have to have a sexual relationship! We can just live together, be together, just brother and sister, with Carrie too. Please, please, *I beg you not to marry Paul!*"[8]

Catherine doesn't listen, of course. Before the book's end she has married not only Paul but Julian as well, who dies in a car accident after impregnating her. Cathy doesn't marry Bart, but she does have an affair with him before the flaming climax, which includes Bart dying in the ashes of doomed Foxworth Hall. Cathy, now pregnant with Bart's child, marries Paul, who doesn't live long either (he has heart problems). Another highlight of the plot of *Petals* includes Carrie's suicide by eating arsenic-powdered doughnuts—the same method by which her twin, Cory, had been murdered.

Cathy comes of age in this book, but it is hard to see much maturation. The only evidence of her supposed maturity is that she drops the use of the girlish expressions seen in the first book, such as "Golly-lolly," and "Good golly day." She has become man-hungry, almost mercilessly seducing her targeted lovers, Paul out of uncontrolled lust and Bart out of revenge.

The revenge theme is strong in *Petals*. Cathy is obsessed with thoughts of revenge. In contrast, her brother Chris gets on with his life, concentrating on college and medical school, with only brief time-outs for pursuing his sister romantically. The emotions of revenge and passion that drive Cathy during this period of her life are a scary combination. At one point, her old dance teacher screams, "*You got something eating at you, Catherine! Something gnawing at your guts. Something so bitter it simmers in your eyes and grits your teeth together! I know your kind. You ruin everyone who touches your life and God help the next man who loves you as much as my son did!*" (*Petals*, 303).

Bart Winslow's seduction is a perfect way for Cathy to combine the driving forces of both lust and revenge. Attracted to her mother's young husband ever since she saw him dozing in *Flowers*, Cathy is sure that seducing Corrine's husband is perfect retaliation against her despised mother. Cathy resembles her mother physically; she is young and is not bound by the conditions of a hateful old man's will; and she can have children. Thus Cathy figures that her appearance as a fresh, young, fertile version of her mother should prove irresistible to Bart. Since most of the characters in Andrews's books tend to be weak in the morals arena, Cathy succeeds easily. (For Foxworth relationships, see Figure 1, page 27.)

This volume in the Dollanganger series includes one of the most grotesque scenes V. C. Andrews ever wrote. Toward the end of the book, Cathy—revenge eating at her relentlessly—sneaks into Foxworth Hall, where the old grandmother lies in bed, immobilized by a stroke. Cathy, dressed in full dance regalia, taunts, rants, and raves at the old woman and at one point even dances on the bed over the grandmother. She then decides to ruin the old woman's hair, as the grandmother had once poured tar on Cathy's golden Dresden-doll locks. Having no tar handy, Cathy settles for hot candle wax and lets some drip on the woman's head before even Cathy starts to see how ludicrously she is behaving.

At the end of *Petals* Cathy is still relatively young, not out of her twenties. What an event-filled life, with more to come—no wonder these books became best-sellers and continue to sell well in the stores. Indeed, many stores stock all V. C. Andrews titles, not just a selection of titles, as is done with the works of most other best-selling authors.

Publication of this book resulted in one of the kindest reviews Andrews ever received: Bea Maxwell stated in the *Los Angeles Times,* "Although certain situations tax credibility, this pop novel of suspense and romance skillfully ensnares. Andrews lulls the reader, then shocks and awakens. The power of evil is pervasive; when there are glimpses of goodness, they warm like sunshine."[9]

If There Be Thorns

You would think the reading public had had enough of the incest-haunted, guilt-ridden Foxworths—but no. In 1981, a year after publication of *Petals,* the third book in the Dollanganger series was published: *If There Be Thorns.* This book departs from the format of the earlier ones. Whereas Cathy had been the narrator of the first two books, making it easy for female readers to identify with her, in *Thorns* the story is told by Cathy's two young sons, Jory and Bart. Jory, at 14, is the son of Cathy's first husband, Julian, and he, like his father, is headed for a career as a dancer. Bart, aged 9, the son of Bart Winslow, had a complicated birth, and Cathy can have no more children.

That's probably a good thing, for lo and behold, Cathy and her sons are living in Marin County, California, with Cathy's new husband, Christopher "Sheffield." A new adopted daughter, Cindy, soon joins the family circle. Jory and Bart have been told a cockamamy story about their parents' past lives, and since the little family now lives a continent away in hidden, fog-shrouded hills, one might hope the awful secret of the Foxworths could be put to rest. That is not, of course, to be.

Naturally, there is an old deserted mansion in the neighborhood, and guess who moves in? A mysterious old woman and her sinister butler. They are intriguing to Jory and Bart, and the old woman seems fascinated by Bart. Bart is the old woman's grandson and the son of her second husband, for she is Corrine, Cathy's hated mother. Corrine has arrived on the scene with the old family butler, John Amos, to make contact with Bart, to read her father's diary, and to get morbid about religion.

Faithful readers of the series by now know many of the secrets of the Foxworths. But, it seems, there are always a few more tidbits to drop into the whole mess to make it all the more titillating. In this book we learn that Corrine's first husband and father of the Dollanganger children was not Corrine's half-uncle but her half-brother. Corrine's father, mean old Malcolm, had raped his beautiful young widowed stepmother, which act resulted in a child, Corrine. Corrine had been passed off as Olivia's child, while the stepmother and her son, Christopher, were ruthlessly tossed out of Foxworth Hall.

Grandmother Corrine has arrived on the scene for what appear to be rather fuzzy reasons. Because she is determined to turn Bart against his own mother, revenge against Cathy for having seduced her second husband may be a strong motivation. It would seem that mother and daughter are very similar indeed, not only in appearance but also in emotional makeup. The scene of confrontation between Cathy and Corrine is a beauty:

> "Mother!" she screamed. "I should have known months ago it was you. From the moment I entered this house I sensed your presence, your perfume, the colors, the choice of furniture. You had sense enough to cover your face and body in black, but you were stupid enough to wear your jewelry. Dumb, always so damned dumb! Is it insanity, or is it stupidity that makes you think I could forget your perfume, your jewelry?" She laughed, wild and hysterically, spinning around and around so John Amos, who was trying to prevent what she might do, was stumbling, clumsily trying to grab hold of her before she could attack again.[10]

The scene goes on, somewhat reminiscent of Cathy's dancing over her sick grandmother's prone body:

> Look at her—she was dancing! All around my grandmother she whirled, flicking out her hand to slap at her—and even as she whipped her legs around, she screamed: "I should have known

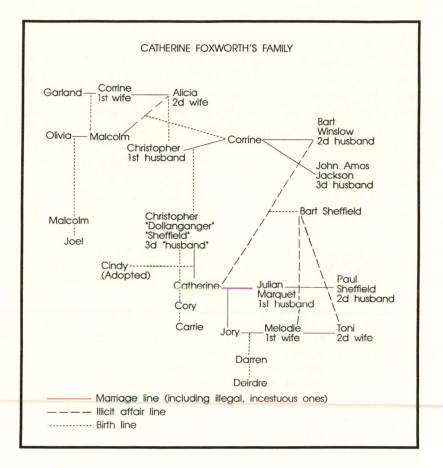

CATHERINE FOXWORTH'S FAMILY

Marriage line (including illegal, incestuous ones)
Illicit affair line
Birth line

it was you. Ever since you moved in Bart has been acting crazy. You couldn't leave us alone, could you? You had to come here and try and ruin what Chris and I have together—the first time we've been happy. And now you've ruined it. You've managed to drive Bart insane so he'll have to be put away like you were. Oh, how I hate you for that. How I hate you for so many reasons." (*Thorns*, 308)

The device of using two boys to narrate the story rather than Cathy, the usual storyteller, is not as effective as one might like. It does, however, have the advantage of allowing the reader to rediscover all those family horrors through innocent new eyes. And, of course, the new twists and details make avid fans happy and hungry for more. Some details seem hard to believe, such as John Amos's insistence that he has married Corrine, but all things are possible in a V. C. Andrews novel. Even the ending, with yet another mansion burning and Corrine dying in a final act of saving Cathy's life, is possible, if not believable.

About this book one reviewer commented:

> Andrews' forte may not be understatement, but she does weave an absorbing narrative around the staple items of pulp literature. Even without the benefit of hindsight from Andrews' earlier books, . . . the two brothers who contribute the strange narrative to "Thorns" emerge as credible (if pitiable) characters.
> All this has the fascination of screaming tabloid headlines. That may explain why both of Andrews' previous novels were best sellers. People enjoy the redemptive suffering of others— it's a great relief when these things happen to someone else.[11]

In considering the first three books of the Dollanganger saga, one can see that Andrews's title for the original manuscript, *The Obsessed*, was a good one, very descriptive of the plot. The fast publication of these first three titles and the strong ties of characters and themes would seem to indicate that these three books were the body of that first version. No more Dollanganger books were to appear until 1984. For a few years it seemed that the Dollanganger story was complete, and reviewers spoke of the Dollanganger trilogy as a set. But the faithful were finally rewarded, for the series did indeed continue. And although another book by V. C. Andrews had appeared during the hiatus, the Dollanganger saga remained the favorite of most of her readers.

Seeds of Yesterday

Seeds of Yesterday, published in March 1984, brings Cathy Foxworth's story to an end. For the literal minded who like to compare dates and ages, the only way for Cathy now to be in her fifties would be to have the story taking place in the near future. Cathy was born in 1945 and is 15 when she escapes from the attic in 1960. Andrews is careful in her books to keep references to current events at a minimum, however, and so an alternate to having *Seeds* take place in the future is to accept that time has somehow telescoped, the way it frequently does in television soap operas. Certainly, current events are seldom allowed to intrude on the plot—for example, one might wonder how the older Christopher, sire of the Dollanganger children, managed to avoid military service during the 1940s. At any rate, it is the story that counts with Andrews's books; the time frame is unimportant. It is the characters who make the plot move, not outside world events.

The plot of *Seeds* pulls a number of threads together in the Dollanganger series. Foxworth Hall has been reconstructed to resemble the original as much as possible, and Bart, heir to the Foxworth fortune, is soon to come into his legacy at the age of 25. He has summoned the family to the old/new family site to help him celebrate. Chris, Cathy, and Cindy plan to stay awhile before making a new home in Hawaii (apparently California wasn't far enough away to escape). Jory, now a successful dancer, arrives with his pregnant wife, Melodie, Bart's lust object. Completing the family scene is a long-lost member of the clan, thought dead for years: Joel Foxworth, Corrine's brother, who had run away from his awful parents and was reported to have perished in a Alpine snowslide in his youth. Instead, he has been living in a monastery but now is happy to be back. Just why is anybody's guess.

Although *Seeds* has a somewhat slower pace, lots of catastrophes and passion pop up all over the place. For some reason all those years in the monastery didn't do Joel much good in the human-kindness department, for he skulks around nastily, doing horrid mischief and causing serious accidents. His major coup happens early on, with the crippling of Jory, thereafter condemned to life in a wheelchair. Jory's wife, Melodie, cannot cope with this situation and has an affair with Bart before giving birth to twins, little clones of Cory and Carrie. This time they are called Darren and Deirdre. Melodie finally leaves, going back to her own career as a dancer. A beautiful nurse is hired for Jory; she first has an affair with Bart before learning to love Jory. Bart and Cindy fight and wrangle constantly. But in the end, Bart and Cindy both get religion, with Bart becoming a famous television evangelist and Cindy embarking on a career as a Hollywood actress. Joel finally dies of cancer; Chris is killed by a car; and Cathy dies peacefully staring out a window in the attic. Her family discovers the journals Cathy has been writing all these years, which accounts for the Dollanganger narrative in the first place.

Certain motifs are repeated in the Dollanganger series. Andrews refers to history repeating itself, and basic fears about inheriting traits from older generations recur among the characters. For example, there is even a hint that things might still not be over, for old Joel tries to lay a guilt trip on Darren and Deirdre:

> "Now, children who have not learned how to control physical demands, repeat the lessons I have tried to teach you. Speak, and tell me, Darren, Deirdre! Speak the words you are supposed to keep forever in your minds and hearts. Speak, and let God hear."
>
> They had such babyishly small voices that seldom said more than a few words at a time. They sometimes used the wrong syntax . . . but this time they intoned as correctly and as seriously as adults. . . .
>
> "We are the children born of evil seed. We are the Devil's issue, the Devil's spawn. We have inherited all the evil genes that lead to inces—incestuous relationships."
>
> Pleased with themselves, they grinned at each other for hav-

ing said it right, not understanding in the least the meaning of the words.[12]

As with Andrews's earlier books, there were mixed reviews of this new title in the series, with one critic referring to Chris and Cathy's "husband-and-wife fantasy" and the judgment that "it's hard to figure why everyone acts so creepy."[13] The reviewer in this case didn't seem to grasp V. C. Andrews's basic appeal to her readers: *why* people act creepy is of no concern; it's enough that they *do* act creepy. Another reviewer remarked, "Credit must be given, though: after all the evil, illness, insanity and devastation already visited on the family, Andrews comes up with further punishments even if they recall the Bible less than the *National Enquirer* or *Stella Dallas*. Added to this are object lessons on wealth and true love overcoming all.[14]

Other reviewers grudgingly gave faint praise, such as one who said, "Virginia Andrews' writing is embarrassingly crude and naive, especially in her first books, though she has improved greatly in the course of writing four. . . . But there is strength in her books—the bizarre plots, matched with the pathos of the entrapped, which she herself clearly feels."[15]

Garden of Shadows

The last entry in the Dollanganger series is a sort of prelude to the real story, for the Dollanganger children have not yet been born. *Garden of Shadows* was published in 1987, a few months after V. C. Andrews's death. The copyright is given as her legal incorporation, as was the case with several of her previous books, and so it is reasonable to suppose she completed the book before her death. The story is shorter, however, and although the page count is similar to that in her earlier books, *Garden* has been set in larger type. The writing style, too, seems a bit different, marked by shorter sentences and a less descriptive approach to the narrative. It may be that a ghostwriter was involved in the project. A publisher's note in another posthumously published book, *Dark Angel,* states that Andrews was a prolific author and at the time of her death had a number of completed manuscripts that would be published in the future. In the last sketch on her in *Contemporary Authors* is a comment that she had composed brief synopses for an additional 63 books.[16]

Her death was not loudly trumpeted by her publisher. The obituaries were brief and appeared in the expected places, but the publisher did nothing that might make the blitzkreig of V. C. Andrews book sales falter.

Garden is the story of Olivia, the cruel grandmother. It begins in Connecticut, where Olivia is an unmarried, businesslike woman involved in her father's financial empire. She is reconciled to the life of a spinster because of her large size and lack of beauty, but then Malcolm Foxworth arrives on the scene. Malcolm treats Olivia to a whirlwind courtship and sweeps her away to his mansion in Virginia, where he expects her to be as helpful to him as she has been to her father.

Malcolm's incredibly poor style in the bedroom and his general lack of sensitivity quickly show Olivia the joyless kind of life she faces. The birth of two sons offers some consolation; however, more trouble is on the horizon: Malcolm's father suddenly arrives with a beautiful, new, and pregnant second wife. Malcolm obviously hates this situation, but Olivia tries to deal with it as best she can, although she knows the servants find her cold and heartless in comparison with the new Mrs. Foxworth.

The sexual relationship between Garland Foxworth and his young wife is a matter of great fascination for both Malcolm and Olivia. Despite the age difference, Garland and Alicia obviously have a very erotic, sexually satisfying relationship. Malcolm knows they do because he spies on their lovemaking through a hole in their bedroom wall; Olivia, because she lurks in the bushes watching all in an alfresco mating.

It may be that finding out what she's been missing all these years further embitters Olivia to the point of psychosis, for she becomes hard, sanctimonious, merciless, and cruel. The story, told in Olivia's words, claims she still loves her sons and the baby, Corrine, who is posing as one of her children. Yet Olivia has little tolerance for human frailties, and her patience is quickly exhausted in dealing with her growing children.

As the story progresses, Garland dies. Alicia and her son, Christopher, are turned away from Foxworth Hall, and Alicia later dies, leaving Christopher, at age 17, to the mercy of his ruthless relatives. He arrives at the mansion, and although things go well enough at first, Olivia begins to see Corrine as a weak, indulgent girl who is becoming much too attached to the young man she believes is her half-uncle.

Despite Olivia's efforts to make people behave themselves, tragedy strikes. Malcolm Jr. is killed in a motorcycle accident (a switch from a car accident, at least), and Joel runs away and is thought to have died in a snowslide in Switzerland. The inevitable happens, and Olivia discovers Chris and Corrine cavorting in the beautiful swan bed where Garland had once made love to her husband's mother (who had deserted early on, causing Malcolm to turn into a misogynist) and where he later coupled with the stunning Alicia. This is also the bed on which Malcolm raped Alicia in her widowhood.

Chris and Corrine leave, not to be heard of again until the closing pages of *Garden,* when Olivia permits Corrine and her children to return to Foxworth Hall, the children becoming the "flowers in the attic."

Incest as a Theme
in the Dollanganger Series

One of the most fascinating, horrific themes in Andrews's work is that of incest. This is not the incest of child abuse; it is the incest of forbidden lust. The Dollanganger series uses this theme as a recurring motif throughout, though it is not as omnipresent in the prequel as in the four volumes dealing with the Dollanganger children.

Although both voyeurism and adultery occur in the prequel, incest becomes a real part of the Foxworth family's secret only when Corrine and Christopher decide to ignore social, moral, and legal traditions by marrying and having children. When they make this decision, they believe they are half-niece and half-uncle. This particular relationship is one forbidden by law, which states in the Code of Virginia that marriage between an uncle and a niece, whether by half or whole blood, is prohibited.

In addition, those with this relationship who leave the state to marry and then return to Virginia are liable to jail and fine. Pennsylvania law is less specific, forbidding marriage between a full-blood uncle and niece and not referring to the half-blood relationship, although the latter kind of sexual relationship is punishable under a different statute. It is interesting to note that the laws seem more concerned with family psychological relationships than with possible genetic defects of children born of such unions. There is no doubt about the nature of biblical law, however, for Leviticus clearly spells out all the prohibitions in sexual relationships. At any rate, a marriage ceremony entered into by Christopher and Corrine would probably have been done through deceit, without disclosing their blood relationship. Andrews gives no legal details on any marriage ceremonies, civil or otherwise, that may or may not have occurred.

It should be remembered that Christopher Sr. was killed without knowing the truth of the closeness of his relationship with Corrine, and that Corrine discovered it only after reading about it in Malcolm's journal in her old age. It might have made no difference had they known. As is constantly being pointed out in the Dollanganger books, when love is so strong, how can it be wrong? And so it is obvious that Christopher and Corrine were willing to defy familial, legal, and religious restrictions in order to seal their relationship by having children.

Old Malcolm and Olivia know the truth of Christopher and Corrine's blood relationship. As a reformed sinner, Malcolm is a proper Bible thumper, and self-righteousness seems to come naturally to Olivia. It's a wonder these two did not turn Christopher and Corrine over to the authorities, yet we cannot discount the power of southern family honor in these situations. Disowning the runaway lovers seems rather mild as a punishment, considering the magnitude of the sin.

Evidently because of a good gene pool, none of the Dollanganger children are mentally defective (unless one counts general Foxworth nuttiness), and only Carrie suffers physically with stunted growth. In the books this disability is accounted for by Carrie's imprisonment in the attic during important growth years; still, one can't help but wonder.

At any rate, by the time the next generation gets into the incest act, Chris, as a budding doctor, apparently knows the dangers of playing genetic dice. One is not so sure of Cathy's good sense in this respect, for she generally displays little sensibility, even in the best of times. Although she originally planned never to have children, in order to devote herself to her dance career, she lets temper and passion get in the way most of the time, and there is never any mention of birth control measures being taken. That she has two children indicates her original resolve to have none was obviously not strong.

The question of genetic danger to possible offspring aside, Andrews seems more interested in using incest—or sin of any kind, along with its accompanying guilt—as a punishment in itself. The consequences of sin are not necessarily the obvious results but, rather, in the sin repeating itself with others—a sort of genetic defect showing itself as an inherited moral weakness passing from one generation to another. Andrews may also have felt that the possible guilt accompanying sin is punishment in itself. The older Christopher and Corrine, however, do not seem to be overcome with guilt; nor does the younger Chris. And though Cathy broods about it sometimes, her emotions are so tangled that it's often hard to identify what she's feeling guilty about as she rationalizes and defends her various impulsive and premeditated actions.

My Sweet Audrina

Only one of V. C. Andrews's books to date is not part of a longer series: *My Sweet Audrina*. Published in 1982, following the success of the first three Dollanganger titles, *Audrina* may have been written by Andrews during her earlier unpublished years. It has the distinction of being the first of her works to be published as a hardcover, rather than just a mass-market paperback. *Audrina* also quickly became a best-seller and did not disappoint Andrews's fans. The little heroine of this new book, Audrina, had plenty of lurid adventures to keep V. C. Andrews's readers happy.

When the story opens, Audrina is a sheltered child, is not in school, and has no memories of her past. She lives in a beautiful old house in western Virginia with her parents, Aunt Ellsbeth, and her cousin Vera. There had once been an older sister whose name had been Audrina too, but she is dead, after a brutal gang rape in the mysterious woods nearby. Audrina's father is a sinister figure, and Audrina cannot understand what he wants from her. She fears he is trying to coax the ghostly spirit of the first Audrina to possess her and have both Audrinas united in one body.

In this strange house are many secrets. Audrina's mother and aunt hold tea parties with a long-dead great-aunt, Mercy Marie. Audrina's cousin Vera has a mean spirit. It comes as no surprise that Vera is really Audrina's half-sister, the product of Audrina's father's earlier indiscretion. Audrina meets a boy, Arden, in the forbidden woods. He takes her home to meet his mother, who turns out to be a legless former skating star. Audrina's mother becomes pregnant but dies with the birth of Sylvia, who is beautiful but mentally deficient. Audrina's father marries Arden's mother; Vera runs away to a probable life of sin and shame; and Audrina finally discovers there never was a dead older Audrina—she is the only Audrina.

After further melodrama, Audrina and Arden grow up and seem to have a relatively normal love for each other. In the final pages of the story, Audrina decides to leave her decadent home behind. She will also leave behind her father, who will be at the mercy of erratic Sylvia. Yet in the end Audrina cannot go, and she stays with her strange and demanding family. This is Audrina's destiny.

Publication of this book elicited the snarling fangs of some critics: "Does a sensible reader really want to know more? The writing is execrable. Most of the brief sexual passages involve third parties watching in fascination, which gives things a little spin, I suppose. Nothing else makes much sense."[17]

Perhaps things didn't make much sense to the *New York Times* reviewer, but Andrews's readers loved *Audrina* anyhow. In many ways this book is the most steeped in southern Gothic atmosphere and feeling, for the special relationship between Audrina and her father is very southern. It is Audrina's father who dominates the novel, inspiring Audrina's love/hate feelings for him. Even in the end she cannot leave him. To quote Florence King, a wry commentator on the southern scene, "Even the best Southern women novelists cannot keep their fingers off those magic keys, f-a-t-h-e-r. Margaret Mitchell gave us not one but two idyllic father-daughter relationships. The healthier was that of Scarlett and Gerald O'Hara; the bond between Rhett Butler and Bonnie gave every promise of becoming a classically sick Electra mess prevented only by the child's untimely death."[18]

The Heaven Series

Heaven

In 1985 a new series started. The first title was *Heaven* and introduced the Casteels, a troubled family in West Virginia. Heaven Leigh, the central character of this book and the two immediately following, is beautiful and good. Heaven's mother had not been a mountain girl; as a girl of 14 from a wealthy New England family she had fallen madly in love with Thomas Luke Casteel. The lovely girl was not hardy enough for mountain life, though, and died when Heaven was born.

Heaven's father needs a new wife. He makes Sarah Heaven's stepmother, and Sarah in time becomes the mother of Heaven's four half-brothers and half-sisters. Since Granny and Grandpa still live with the Casteels, the little mountain cabin is crowded. Heaven takes to daydreaming of her rich relatives up north, hoping things will somehow get better in her life.

Mountain girls grow up fast, and when Heaven meets Logan

Stonewall she is sure he is the one man for her, even if she is only 13. The only trouble is that Heaven's stepsister Fanny also thinks Logan is for her, and Fanny is a loose, immoral girl.

Then Sarah, the Casteel children's anchor, leaves, tired of her mean, unfaithful husband. Old Granny has always said that Thomas Luke Casteel buried his finer qualities with his beloved first wife and had only his bad qualities left. Heaven's father has just begun to show his children his true meanness.

Thomas Luke Casteel decides to liquidate his assets, and the only ones he has are his bright, attractive children. He sells the Casteel youngsters to eager adoptive parents, splitting up Heaven, Tom Jr., Fanny, Keith, and Our Jane. Heaven's father lets her choose her new family, and she picks Cal and Kitty Dennison, who take her away from everyone and everything she loves, including her beautiful mountains.

Heaven's new life in Atlanta is far from a wonderful dream. Her foster parents are odd; Kitty wants to revenge herself on Heaven's parents, and Cal wants Heaven's body. Heaven is growing up, and she desires Cal as much as he wants her. Kitty becomes an invalid, and Heaven and Cal become lovers.

On a return trip to the mountains to visit Kitty's ailing mother, Heaven sees Logan again and finds her old feelings for him unchanged. She hears from her father, who has remarried and wants to find his children. Yet Heaven has formed a new obsession: she wants to meet and know her mother's Boston family. At the book's end Heaven leaves for Boston to satisfy this yearning.

Dark Angel

The story of Heaven Leigh Casteel continues in *Dark Angel,* published in 1986. Now in Boston with her wealthy grandmother and her handsome stepgrandfather, Tony Tatterton, Heaven is sure at first that her childhood dreams of another, better life have come true. But as readers of Andrews's other books could predict with surety, Heaven is not going to have a peaceful time of it in New England.

Heaven is sent to exclusive Winterhaven, where she meets rich girls her own age. These girls do not become her friends; rather, they merely reinforce Heaven's feelings of insecurity and inferiority. In a small secluded house behind her grandmother's mansion, Farthinggale, she finds Tony's much-younger brother Troy. Logan turns up in Boston, but now it is Troy who fascinates Heaven.

Heaven is still in touch with her mountain family. Fanny is pregnant and penniless; Tom Jr. is being exploited by their father; and the two youngest are still happy with their foster parents. Heaven decides to track down her family before marrying Troy, and she finds her brother Tom working in a tacky circus their father now runs. Fanny has sold her child to her foster parents and is trying to break into show biz in Nashville, but she finally tires of struggling for success and marries a rich old man.

Back in her mountain village, Heaven comes across both Cal Dennison and Logan Stonewall. On her return to Boston, Heaven learns an awful truth from Tony: that Thomas Luke Casteel is not her biological father; Tony is. This means that marriage with Troy, her half-brother, is out of the question. Troy, crazed with unhappiness, rides a reckless horse into the ocean, supposedly never to be seen again.

Heaven returns to the mountains, where there are hints of a renewed romance with Logan. Young Tom Jr. is killed by circus cats. Tom Sr. is badly injured trying to save him. Fanny continues to be selfish. Heaven is still confused over her identity.

When *Dark Angel* was published it took only three days for the book to become number one on the national best-seller list. Andrews's touch in telling stories about strange yet glamorous people had not faltered. She admitted to writing about people who are kinky, but she did not feel she herself was kinky in any way. The new series about the Casteel clan seemed destined to popularity almost equal to that accorded the Foxworths.

Fallen Hearts

In the third book of the Casteel family series, *Fallen Hearts,* Heaven is back in her old hometown, has a new career as a teacher in the village school, and is engaged to Logan Stonewall. She has also dyed her dark hair blond, making her a look-alike for her dead mother. The dye job also makes Heaven seem even more like Cathy Foxworth of the Dollanganger series. (It should be noted that Virginia Andrews herself had blond hair.)

Heaven is not, however, fated to spend the rest of her life in such wholesome simplicity. After she and Logan are married, they fly to Boston and let Tony host an elaborate reception and honeymoon for them at Farthinggale. Heaven's grandmother Jillian is insane but not locked away anywhere; instead, she drifts from her room periodically in order to embarrass the family at social gatherings. Heaven is still haunted by the memory of Troy. Tony easily persuades Logan to give up his career as a pharmacist and become his assistant, concentrating on building a new factory in the mountains where local artisans can create new Tatterton toys. Heaven quits her teaching job.

Heaven and Logan jet between their old mountain home and their new home at Farthinggale. Fanny, ever interested in new conquests, throws herself at Logan. Heaven discovers that Troy isn't dead and is still around the Farthinggale estate. Heaven spends a night of illicit love with Troy, and Logan is easily seduced by Fanny. Troy runs away. Jillian dies. Heaven and Fanny are both pregnant, and no one is really sure who the father of either child is.

Heaven's mountain father, Luke, and his wife are killed in a car crash; Heaven and Logan take in their son, Drake, who is nominally Heaven's half-brother. Tony tries to rape Heaven, who returns to the mountains with Logan and Drake. Heaven dyes her hair back to its original dark shade. Fanny snatches Drake, probably to be spiteful, and gets her current young boyfriend to marry her. After an extremely nasty custody trial over Drake, Heaven gives Fanny $1 million to get him. Fanny and Heaven have their babies on the same day—Fanny a boy, Luke, who looks like Logan, and Heaven a girl, Annie, who looks like Heaven.

Gates of Paradise

As the story of the Casteel family progresses in the next book of the series, *Gates of Paradise,* the family narration is picked up by Heaven's daughter, Annie, now a teenager. Annie, Drake, and

Luke have grown up together, but Annie and Luke's love for each other is not brotherly and sisterly. Their closeness is a forbidden love, for Logan is probably the father of both.

The dashing Fanny has a birthday party. Logan drinks too much at the party and crashes the car on the drive home. Logan and Heaven are killed in the accident, and Annie is temporarily crippled. Tony Tatterton arrives on the scene, sweeping Annie away to Farthinggale and luring Drake into his web by promising him the opportunity to be a member of the Tatterton Corporation.

Annie's recovery is slow but spicy, as her nurse, Mrs. Broadbent, exhibits lesbian tendencies, and Tony seems very confused over Annie's real identity. He persuades her to dye her hair blond, further confusing him as to whether she is Annie, Heaven, Leigh, or Jillian—Tony seems to be lusting after all these women. Troy is still lurking in the cottage beyond the maze, still as melancholy as young Werther in Goethe's famous Gothic novel. Faithful Luke is kept from Annie by Tony through deceit and lies.

Finally Annie escapes from Tony and Farthinggale, returning to the mountains and what appears to be a genuine love from her Aunt Fanny. Annie and Luke become more and more enamored of each other, discovering, fortunately, that Annie's biological father was not Logan but Troy. Tony dies, still confused, and Troy blesses the two young lovers, Annie and Luke.

Web of Dreams

This final volume in the Casteel series is similar to the last in the Dollanganger series, in that it is a prequel, picking up loose threads of the overall story. In the prologue we find that Annie has come to Farthinggale for Troy's internment and discovers a diary written by her grandmother Leigh. This book, then, is Leigh's story.

Leigh had been a shadowy figure in the earlier books of the series. We discover she is the daughter of a beautiful and selfish woman, almost a dead ringer for Corrine Foxworth. Leigh's mother, Jillian, has provided a lovely home for Leigh with the man Leigh thinks is her father, an old-salt type who owns luxury ocean liners. Jillian anxiously pushes Leigh to grow up, and when

Leigh is 12 Jillian divorces the old salt and marries rich, young, and handsome Tony Tatterton, who is unaware of Jillian's true age. Leigh discovers that the old salt is not her biological father and begins to look at Jillian through less-than-rosy-hued glasses.

Jillian is obsessed with losing her beauty, and Tony becomes increasingly interested in the maturing Leigh, another beautiful blond Andrews heroine. The old salt marries a woman named Mildred Pierce (the name of the heroine in a beloved 1940s movie), and Leigh finds herself trusting only Tony's little brother, Troy.

Tony wants Leigh, at 13, to pose nude for him as a model for an expensive new line of portrait dolls, and Jillian encourages Leigh to do as Tony wants. Tony's interest in Leigh becomes more and more evident and culminates in her rape during the absence of Jillian, who has gone to a Swiss health spa. Jillian, on her return, is unbelieving and uncaring about Leigh's story. When Leigh realizes she is pregnant, she flees from Farthinggale to seek help from her grandmother in Texas.

On a layover in Atlanta she meets and falls in love with Thomas Luke Casteel, who in turn is hopelessly smitten with Leigh. They marry quickly (with no questions asked by the justice of the peace) and travel to Luke's home in West Virginia to await the birth of Leigh's child, who will be named Heaven.

V. C. Andrews as a Writer

V. C. Andrews's writing style has been amply criticized. There is a crude force to some of it, however, that gives it occasional strength. This power is somewhat at odds with the soap-opera quality of most of Andrews's writing but does illustrate her willingness to treat subjects other than passion and greed.

Two instances stand out. One occurs in *Petals in the Wind,* when Cathy dramatically hemorrhages during her dance audition. This is the ultimate bad dream of the many teenage girls who dread the thought of menstrual blood showing through their clothes. The other occurs in *Dark Angel,* when Heaven is played a dirty trick by the girls of her exclusive girls' school. She is slipped a fast-acting, powerful laxative during a party and then finds all the bathrooms locked when the inevitable happens. Resourceful Heaven improvises and ultimately gets back at the perpetrators of the trick; nevertheless, the incident reveals another secret fear of many—that of having to deal with embarrassing bodily functions in difficult circumstances. Both instances show that Andrews was willing to deal with adolescent insecurities, as well as the concerns of the heart.

"V. C. Andrews" Today

It is strongly rumored that the last two titles in the Heaven series were written by Andrew Neiderman, himself a published writer of horror books.[19] Although it is entirely possible that Andrews plotted a number of books before her death, careful examination of the last few shows a lack of attention to detail that she herself would never have allowed. In the last title, for example, throughout the course of the book Leigh is given pendants by three different people important to her. In each case she is thrilled and happy, yet nowhere is it told what becomes of the pendants given to her earlier. Perhaps she no longer wears them or has thrown them away in anger, but the reader is never told. Anachronisms, too, crop up here and there, as when the word *unisex* appears in a story obviously taking place in the mid-1950s, long before the term was in popular use.

The publication of *Dawn,* the first book in a new series started in 1990, includes the following note to the reader from the Andrews family:

> Since her [V. C. Andrews's] death many of you have written to us wondering whether there would continue to be new V. C. Andrews novels. When Virginia became seriously ill while writing the Casteel series, she began to work even harder, hoping to finish as many stories as possible so that her fans could one day share them. Just before she died we promised ourselves

that we would take all of these wonderful stories and make them available to her readers.

Beginning with the final books in the Casteel series we have been working closely with a carefully selected writer to organize and complete Virginia's stories and to expand upon them by creating additional novels inspired by her wonderful storytelling genius.[20]

Despite questions about who is really writing V. C. Andrews's books now, her works are still very popular. Her books have been translated into 13 foreign languages, as well as being published in other English-speaking countries.

Flowers in the Attic: The Movie

To date, only one of Andrews's books—*Flowers in the Attic*—has been made into a movie. Plans for a film based on this book were under way before her death. She was most interested in the project and had a number of ideas regarding casting, such as having Bea Arthur (best known for her roles in the television series "Maude" and "The Golden Girls") play the cruel grandmother.

In the end the film was cast with other actors: Louise Fletcher as the grandmother, Victoria Tennant as Corrine, Kristy Swanson as Cathy, and Jeb Stuart Adams as Chris. Released in 1988, the film received what at best could be called mixed reviews and rather poor box-office profits. In its second release, this time on video for the home market, the film performed better financially. Since a lot of teens enjoy renting videos and having video parties at home, *Flowers* may be playing to its best audience at last.

The film was remarkably faithful to the spirit of the book, particularly in creating a good spooky mood. The colors are reminiscent of turn-of-the-century decadence: dark, murky tones of deep reds and browns. The background music is always in a minor key. The plot was changed somewhat, primarily to increase its melodrama, one supposes, with the most blatant change occurring at the end. After Cory's death from poison, the frantic children walk out of their attic and confront their mother at the altar while she is marrying Bart Winslow. In the highly emotional scene, Corrine backs away from the belligerent Cathy and falls into an arbor. Her white wedding veil catches on a broken slat, and Corrine is hanged by her own wedding finery.

In one of the most extensive reviews of the film, Harry Mc-Cracken, writing in *Cinefantastique,* judges that

> despite everything, FLOWERS IN THE ATTIC gets under your skin. Slowly and methodically—and without any traditional horror-movie shocks or music effects work—the movie constructs an atmosphere of deep unpleasantness. An early sequence in which Corrine [21] removes her blouse in front of her dying father so that her mother can horsewhip her, then again to display her welts to her children, is disturbing in more ways than one can easily count, and representative of the movie's flavor.
>
> . . . In this virtual catalogue of family relationships gone awry, Chris and Cathy's liaison, astonishingly enough, is one of the least mixed-up ones.
>
> The chords that this story strikes are deep and resonant; it's a shame it hits them so clumsily. The film's best sequence is one of the last ones, in which the wraith-like surviving Dollanganger children escape the attic and confront the mother—during the high-society wedding ceremony at which she is about to be remarried. This scene is perversely funny and yet genuinely unsettling, eloquently accomplishes what the rest of FLOWERS IN THE ATTIC never quite does.[22]

That Virginia Andrews enjoyed writing can be deduced from the zestful way she told her stories. A popular writer is often one who has a good story to tell, and Andrews obviously enjoyed sharing her fantasy/dream stories. In addition, there is a sense that she thought it fun to shock people a bit with details of kinkiness and incest. In her own words:

> I step into a universe of my own making, and I am the god. What a sense of power! . . . When I write, I have dependable friends right there, waiting for me. That's my gift. . . .
>
> All my life I thought I was meant to be something special . . . I never knew what it was. Now I have the satisfaction of having my name recognized. And it will live after me.[23]

3. The Horror of Science: The Creations of Dean R. Koontz

An important event occurred early in the nineteenth century during a stormy spell in Switzerland. Shelley and Lord Byron, noted romantic poets and the scandals of polite English society, were in residence with Shelley's mistress, Mary; Byron's physician, John Polidori; and Mary's stepsister, Claire. On that now-famous stormy night, the bored residents of the château challenged one another to compose original ghost stories. Byron's fragment was later taken up by his physician and became part of vampire literature. Mary's effort, however, became the best known of the stories that were born that evening, for her tale was *Frankenstein; or, The Modern Prometheus.*

Frankenstein is a landmark book, for not only did it give birth to the science fiction genre but it also influenced horror literature, by presenting an important theme that would be used time and time again: the scientist who meddles in forbidden things and creates a monster that cannot be controlled. Mary's story also contained a significant element that frequently appears in such stories—the sorrow of the monster in knowing it cannot be truly human.

It has also been suggested that *Frankenstein* is an important piece of feminist literature, for it tells us that all creatures need nurturing:

What makes him monstrous to the female audience is not his lust for revenge or his appetite for violence, which seem to play out the male romance, but instead that he has been made hideous by his creator's unwillingness to nurture. Again and again we are told in the text, especially by the monster, that if someone would just take a little time to attend to his needs, everything would be just fine. Thus the pubescent female can witness this tale of initiation into the anxieties of motherhood with as rapt an attention as her male counterpart, for she wonders if she will be willing to attend to her own biological production.[1]

The story of a man's creation that turns out to be a monster is one that has enthralled readers and movie audiences for generations. Another, later writer, a compatriot of Mary Shelley's, H. G. Wells, delved into scientific themes to create thriller tales of tension and terror, such as *The Island of Dr. Moreau,* published in 1896. These stories from the early days of Gothic literature and science fiction also serve to illustrate the fuzzy boundaries existing between some of the literary genres, for is a story like *Frankenstein* science fiction, or is it horror? To classify all stories that involve science-made monsters as science fiction seems artificial. Why should a story about the Swamp Thing created by a laboratory accident be science fiction when the Swamp Thing's seemingly close relative, the Hulk, is classed as horror fiction because internal human rage brings about the metamorphosis?

Another complication in classifying stories is that a number of authors write in different genres, sometimes deliberately blurring the lines between. An example is Dean R. Koontz, who has become a popular author of best-selling horror and suspense books in the past decade.

Dean R. Koontz:
Is Any Goodness Left in the World?

I am a raving optimist. There are those among us who are vile and wicked, yes, but they're the genetic freaks, the failures in the species. I think for the most part that the human species

Chronology: Dean R. Koontz's Life and Works

1945   Born 9 July in Everett, Pennsylvania, the only child of Ray and Florence Koontz.

1966   Marries Gerda Cerra; wins *Atlantic Monthly* award for story "The Kittens."

1967–1969   Teaches high school English in Pennsylvania.

1968   *Star Quest.*

1972   *Chase.*

1973   *Blood Risk* published under pseudonym Brian Coffey.

1974   *Strike Deep* published under pseudonym Anthony North.

1975   *The Long Sleep* published under pseudonym John Hill; *Dragonfly* published under pseudonym K. R. Dwyer.

1976   *Prison of Ice* published under pseudonym David Axton.

1977   Film *Demon Seed* released.

1979   *The Key to Midnight* published under pseudonym Leigh Nichols.

1980   *The Funhouse* published under pseudonym Owen West.

1985   *The Door to December* published under pseudonym Richard Paige.

1986   Becomes first president of the newly formed Horror Writers of America.

1989   Film *Watchers* released.

is indeed a reflection of something godlike and that within us
is the potential for wonders. I like people.[2]
                                                —Dean R. Koontz

Dean Koontz always meant to be a writer. As a child he wrote
and illustrated his own stories. As a kid he loved to read books
by H. P. Lovecraft, Richard Matheson, and other horror writers.
In college he won a contest sponsored by *Atlantic Monthly* magazine, and his career as an author was launched. Although his
parents were not encouraging to the young would-be writer (his
father was a violent alcoholic), Koontz's wife, Gerda, was. With
her financial and moral support he was able in his twenties to
establish himself as a successful author.

A prolific writer, Koontz had published more than 50 novels by
1990. Although he started his writing career in the field of science
fiction, since 1972 he has written in other genres and mainstream
fiction. Elements of science remain in his work, however, along
with strong themes of suspense and horror. He considers *Chase,*
published in 1972, his first mainstream title and is not terribly
pleased with his earlier science fiction works, with the exception
of *The Flesh in the Furnace* (1972), *Beastchild* (1970), and *Demon
Seed* (1973).[3] *Demon Seed,* his "last" science fiction tale, was
made into a movie—released in 1977—starring Julie Christie and
Fritz Weaver.

In continuing to trace the upward climb of his writing career
Koontz says:

> I believe the best fiction does three things well: tells an involv-
> ing story, makes the reader think, and makes the reader feel.
> *Night Chills,* a story about mind-control and the dangers to
> individual liberty in a high-technology world, received more
> critical notice than any of my books to that point. *The Vision,*
> with a touch of the occult, was the first book of mine to be se-
> lected by major book clubs and to receive a substantial paper-
> back advance, but my real breakthrough came in 1980, with
> *Whispers,* a very long psychological suspense novel dealing
> with the unknowable and often unrecognized effects that we
> have on one another's lives. (*Cont. Au.,* 19:267)

Since the publication of *Whispers,* Koontz's books have regularly hit the best-seller lists, prompting one critic to remark, "The 1980s has been Dean Koontz's decade. He [*sic*] ascendance was gradual like a fog that rolls in over the breakers, creeps in to cover your feet and every [*sic*] so slowly rises to strangle you before you even know it is there. But, of course, it was there all the time; you just didn't see it until it was all around you."[4]

In the earlier years of his writing career Koontz was advised by his agents and editors to use pseudonyms, or pen names, to designate the different styles he was incorporating in his writing. He now feels this was poor advice, even though his advisers assured him that readers want their favorite authors to write in specific styles and are disappointed if an author creates a mood different from what they expect based on previous titles. For example, Koontz used the name Brian Coffey when writing books "done in a lean, fast-paced style that employed an unusual amount of brisk dialogue" (Munster, 6).

In the later years of the 1980s Koontz stopped using pseudonyms, except for the name Leigh Nichols, which had become a good seller on its own. But finally Nichols too was laid to rest, not as dramatically as Stephen King's pseudonym is buried in *The Dark Half* but through an interview between Koontz and Nichols. The tongue-in-cheek interview in the periodical *Horror Show* ends with Nichols's banishment:

Nichols vanishes. Koontz sits back in his favorite armchair and sighs. "Ah," he says, "life is good these days now that I am one." But in the netherworld other cruelly abandoned pseudonyms— Richard Stark, Richard Bachman, and countless more—are plotting with Nichols to haunt Koontz and drive him to ruin.

Three days later, the poltergeist phenomena in the Koontz house has become so violent and unceasing that crossing a room without being clobbered by a flying chair is impossible, dinner is worn more often than eaten, and no one *dares* enter a bathroom. A priest, solicited to perform an exorcism, is stripped naked by malicious spirits, reclothed in a green dress and red wig, and forced to re-enact episodes of *I Love Lucy.*

"Under these circumstances," Koontz tells *The Horror Show,* "it is a bit more difficult than usual to keep to my writing

schedule, though the problem of concentration engendered by
poltergeist activity is nothing compared to the difficulty of getting dressed in the morning when a malevolent spirit is trying
to strangle you to death with your own socks."[5]

Dean and Gerda Koontz now live in southern California, where
he continues to write intriguing stories that jump onto the best-
seller lists. In describing his writing today, he says, "I am a novelist of the fantastic who writes in a realistic vein" (Munster, 26).
In a catching-up, almost-apologetic way, a number of his earlier
novels published under pseudonyms are now being reissued under the writer's real name, probably more in an effort to cash in
on Koontz's growing reputation than in an effort to set the record
straight.

His early work as a science fiction writer can still be seen in
his writing today. Not only did he sharpen his writing skills in
those early years, but the fascination for certain scientific themes
continues to be present in his more recent books. Although it
seems clear in Koontz's mind that *Demon Seed* was his last science fiction book, it is not so clear to others, for *Demon Seed* presents a horrific theme in futuristic terms—the idea that a
powerful computer wishes to have progeny with a human woman.
We cannot help but wonder what real difference exists between a
monster sired by a devil and one sired by a machine.

The Door to December

One of the books published under the pseudonym Richard Paige,
The Door to December, tells the story of a kidnapped child, Melanie McCaffrey, who is finally reunited with her mother, Laura.
Laura, believing Melanie was with her father, had hoped for the
best during the strained years her little girl was missing. But
when Melanie is found, she is changed: her mind has been altered. Laura discovers that her estranged husband had indeed
been taking care of Melanie, but not as a loving father should.
Instead, he had used her for his experiments in behavior modifi-

cation, and Melanie is now nearly catatonic. Melanie has become a sort of channeler of great psychic energy that she can use to kill. There are, obviously, interesting moral questions to consider in a situation like this, as well as a fast-moving plot that keeps the reader racing through the book to learn what will happen. In the end Koontz's optimism prevails, and there is hope for a return to normalcy for Melanie. This, certainly, is a more positive ending than that of *Altered States,* by Paddy Chayefsky, in which the scientist dooms himself with his mind-altering experiments.

Two other books by Dean Koontz fall more easily into the horror genre because of supernatural elements present in the stories: *Darkfall* and *Phantoms.*

Darkfall

Published in 1984, *Darkfall* tells a story of urban horror, with nasty things biting people to death. A major character in the novel is an appealing 11-year-old girl, Penny Dawson, whose father, Jack, is a police detective investigating the weird deaths. At first Jack believes the deaths are caused by rats—after all, rats are real and have been known to kill people. But Penny is not bound by such conventional thinking, and it is she who is sure that goblins, not rats, are doing the killing, on orders from Baba Lavelle, a powerful voodoo priest. Penny is not bound by what is "real," for, like most children, she knows anything is possible.

Darkfall is a book admired for its pacing.[6] Koontz has a sure hand in knowing when to break an action scene with description, when to end a chapter, and when to switch to another scene. He knows when to lull the reader with a false sense of security and when to shake that same reader awake with terror. For these reasons Dean Koontz has become a popular author with readers, including teens. Without good pacing a story can get bogged down or become confusing; with it, the plot moves along in a calculated way, leading the reader to the end—which, with *Darkfall,* is another mercifully positive Koontz finale. As he explains,

I have no patience whatsoever for misanthropic fiction, of which there is too much these days. In fact, that is one reason why I do not wish to have the "horror novel" label applied to my books even when it is sometimes accurate; too many current horror novels are misanthropic, senselessly bleak, and I do not wish to be lumped with them. I am no Pollyanna, by any means, but I think we live in a time of marvels, not a time of disaster, and I believe we can solve every problem that confronts us if we keep our perspective and our freedom. (*Cont. Au.*, 19:268)

Phantoms

Another tale of supernatural horror is *Phantoms,* published in 1983. In this novel the reader discovers a classic story of good versus evil. This evil is a shape-changing, ancient presence, often seen in the form of a prehistoric, reptilian bird that gorges on human brains. The vile thing has been very busy in a small town in the Sierra Madres, where it has pretty much wiped out the entire population of Snowfield.

Dr. Jenny Paige, who has been away at her mother's funeral, arrives with her innocent young sister, Lisa. Stunned by the carnage surrounding them in Snowfield, they summon the police, who in turn call for help from scientific sources. Good does prevail in the end, but not without a considerable struggle and the final message that we must be ever vigilant to defeat the ancient evil whenever and wherever it appears.

Whispers

One commentator, Michael A. Morrison, suggests that Koontz has created a trilogy with *Darkfall, Phantoms,* and *Whispers,* three books that treat the basic struggle in the human condition between good and evil.[7] The two books already discussed, *Darkfall* and *Phantom,* have evil embodied in a supernatural source. The third book, *Whispers* (1980), has its evil rooted in a different place—the human mind and soul. The imaginary whispers that the dead leave in the minds of the living are as powerful as any supernatural monster or power.

The heroine is Hilary Thomas, a successful California screenwriter who is being subjected to attacks by madman Bruno Frye. Hilary finally kills Bruno, but then he reappears, even though he has been autopsied and buried. Hilary and her lover, police officer Tony Clemenza, face confusion and danger before solving the mystery of Bruno. The evil embodied in Bruno is particularly scary, and the idea that he perhaps cannot be killed is mind-boggling in a novel that does not rely on supernatural explanations for events. Yet as many horror writers know, reality-based terror can be every bit as fearful, if not more so, than occult horror.

In the final scene of *Whispers* Hilary must face Bruno, who is standing above her on the doorstep. She knows that to come closer to Bruno will bring her closer to possible, even probable, death, yet behind her are hordes of cockroaches, "not just ordinary roaches, but enormous things, over two inches long, an inch wide, with busy legs and especially long feelers that quivered anxiously. Their green-brown carapaces appeared to be sticky and wet, like blobs of dark mucous" (*Whispers*, 497-98).

Only a page or two later and Frye is dead, truly dead, at last. Nevertheless, Hilary and the reader know the roaches are still there: you can never totally get rid of roaches.

The Recent Best-sellers

Over the past decade the name Dean Koontz has appeared on the best-seller lists with the same regularity as the name Stephen King. These more recent titles by Koontz tend to be longer, with a more leisurely pace, but also to have well-developed characters, together with the writer's much-admired dialogue. At least one per year has been published to keep Koontz's growing body of fans happy.

Strangers presents a disparate group of characters who seem initially to have only one thing in common—unexplainable bouts of terror and blackouts, these incidents triggered by a variety of things, such as water swirling out of a washbasin. Eventually the different characters discover that each has been brainwashed in some way to forget the night they were all staying at a Nevada motel some months before. All the "strangers" return to the motel, rather like the characters in the film *Close Encounters of the Third Kind* found Devil's Tower. On their return to Nevada the novel's eight major characters learn that the U.S. military has devised a cover-up worthy of the paranoic dreams of any peacemonger.

With *Strangers,* the reviews of Koontz's books became more numerous and more positive, perhaps a result of his growing popularity, but more likely because of his ever-improving ability as a novelist with an exciting story to tell. According to the reviewer in *Booklist,* "Koontz is a true master at constructing vivid, eerily realistic worlds that hold readers spellbound. His latest novel serves up a rich brew of Gothic horror and science fiction, filled with delectable turns of the imagination. . . . A memorable thriller."[8] Another commentator on Dean Koontz's work explains the evolution of his writing as follows:

> In science fiction, it is often the science that takes up the writer's energy. In a sea of robotix and computer chips, alien warriors and post-holocaustal disease, characterization can be left to drift aimlessly. Plots may not be strong enough to hold up under the weight of futuristic technology, which may serve to stretch but also extenuate the imagination.
>
> In horror fiction, on the other hand, we know, or are intimately involved in, the world in which the story is taking place. We therefore care about this world. We can relate more closely to the characters and the emotions they express, and more importantly, so does the author.
>
> By shunting his creative energy from amazing the reader with a futuristic world of technology, Koontz has sharply honed his characterization skills.[9]

Another popular recent title, published in 1987, is *Watchers,* a dog lover's book. The chief character of this title is a superintelligent dog dubbed Einstein by his new foster owner. After being taught to read and write, the dog uses Scrabble tiles to tell his new human friend that The Other, a subject of scientific experiments like Einstein, has escaped and is after Einstein. After a standoff between good (Einstein) and evil (The Other), Koontz lets the good win, leaving every reader wanting a nifty dog like Einstein.

The *Kirkus* reviewer of *Watchers* allowed, "More a fable about love and trust than an outright chiller, this work, with its echoes of *Frankenstein* and *The Island of Dr. Moreau,* still peppers enough tension and mayhem throughout to satisfy horror fans. And the touchy, if often hokey, interplay between dog and human could attract new, non-genre readers. A break-through for Koontz."[10] The *Booklist* reviewer, however, couldn't resist poking fun at the cross-genre nature of the book, calling it a "sci-fi/shaggy-dog/spy/monster/psycho-killer/police-procedural/love story."[11]

Watchers was made into a movie with a boy hero, played by Corey Haim. The story did not work as well in the film as it had in the book, perhaps because "the novel's love story. . . has been replaced with the homey dynamics of a kid . . . and his mom. . . the seminal message of the story are [sic] altered in a crazy quest for a youth-oriented audience."[12]

In *Twilight Eyes* Slim MacKenzie, the young hero, is working in a carnival in the 1960s. Slim is fleeing from his past and trying to avoid his "gift" of "twilight eyes," which gives him the power to see throught the facade of some individuals who are not human beings at all but goblins disguised as human beings. At first Slim thinks the carnival will be a new home, perhaps even a haven for him, particularly when he becomes romantically and sexually involved with his new boss, an attractive young woman. His roving life has prepared him well for life in a carnival, but only too soon he comes to realize that his enemies, the goblins, are plotting a particularly evil scheme of some sort.

Koontz has long been intrigued with carnivals, the setting for *Twilight Eyes,* and says, "Over the years the carnival has continued to fascinate me and I've collected all kinds of background stuff on it."[13] His love for carnivals is evident in the descriptions in this novel.

Koontz's optimistic messages are also apparent in *Twilight Eyes*:

> As I said when I began this story, hope is a constant companion in this life. It is the one thing that neither cruel nature, God, nor other men can wrench from us. Health, wealth, parents, beloved brother and sisters, children, friends, the past, the future—all can be stolen from us as easily as an unguarded purse. But our greatest treasure, hope, remains. It is a sturdy little motor within, purring, ticking, driving us on when reason would suggest surrender. It is both the most pathetic and noblest thing about us, the most absurd and the most admirable quality we possess, for as long as we have hope, we also have the capacity for love, for caring, for decency.[14]

Koontz's next best-seller was *Lightning*, the story of blond, blue-eyed Laura Shane, who, remarkably, is saved by a stranger whenever she is in peril. Lightning strikes, and the mysterious man appears just in the nick of time. The mysterious stranger, Stefan, turns out to be a time-traveling, good Nazi, a man who loves Laura and is determined to save her from danger.

By now Koontz's books are widely reviewed, but it is interesting to see the preoccupation of reviewers in trying to classify him into specific genres—such as this one in *People*: "[Koontz] is billed as 'a grand master of menace,' and the covers of his books are often adorned with lurid, macabre drawings that seem to promise shuddersome shlockiness within. . . . It's fairer to describe him as an author of suspense with supernatural shadings."[15]

With his increasing appearances on the best-seller lists, more reviewers began comparing Koontz with another best-selling horror writer, Stephen King: "But where Stephen King is ebullient and unself-consciously garish, always going for the big effect, Dean Koontz seems more earnest, even a bit plodding, so although his novels . . . offer decent entertainment value for the shocks and shivers crowd, they still lack the dangerous edge that makes Mr. King such a seductive storyteller."[16]

The mad scientist makes an appearance in Dean Koontz's 1989 novel, *Midnight*. People in a small northern California town are being converted to New People, ones without bothersome human emotions. Yet Theodore Shaddock, the villain, cannot stop his New People from regressing into primal beings who kill. Only four people can save the place, and ultimately all of humanity: the pretty heroine seeking the true reason for her sister's death, a world-weary FBI agent, an 11-year-old girl, and a wheelchair-bound Vietnam veteran with a smart dog. Several reviewers commented on the pacing and the well-drawn characters, strengths Koontz has continued to use well in his writing. The protagonists in *Midnight* practice the author's own philosophy of being basically good and decent. As Koontz puts it, "I like people. I think we, as humans, are forever reaching out to others with love and compassion. Humans are constantly advancing, despite terrible, tragic mistakes. And though it seems we always take two steps back for every one step forward—humans consistently *take* that step forward."[17]

As the twentieth century entered its last decade, Dean Koontz published another novel, *The Bad Place*, which went onto the best-seller lists almost immediately. It is another confrontation between good and evil, with the usual sympathetic characters. The side of evil is represented by "a family of genetic misfits with a variety of paranormal powers, . . . and like all really good monsters from Frankenstein's creation to the government experiment Koontz invented in *Watchers*, they inspire at least a modicum of pity" (Graham, 51). The side of good is represented by the Dakotas, a thoroughly nice couple who happen to be private investigators, and by Julie Dakota's brother, Thomas, a psychically gifted victim of Down's syndrome.

The plot is more complex than the capsule description in the *New York Times Book Review* best-seller listing: "A troubled sleepwalker hires detective team to discover the causes and consequences of his behavior."[18] Indeed, there is a darker, grimmer side to *The Bad Place* than is usually the case with Koontz's novels. One reviewer, Michael R. Collings, describes it as here, finally, the subtle undercurrent that makes *The Bad Place* difficult. People die. And not just any people—after all, a novel that is even peripherally related to the horror genre must include some violence. But in *The Bad Place*, the wrong people die. More than in other Koontz novels, the violence is truly unjust. One character—a curmudgeonly doctor-type, at first vaguely reminiscent of Marcus Welby and every other over-the-hill TV doctor—is revealed to be as antisocial as Candy Pollard, a grasping, greedy, self-serving amoral monster. He lives long and prospers. Other, more positive characters, including Thomas, struggle valiantly against afflictions, overcome impossible odds, attract the reader's attention and empathy—and die viciously at the hands of Candy Pollard. There is no justice in the world of *The Bad Place*. As with the internal complexities of genetics and personality development, external events seem controlled by a cosmic Wheel of Fortune.[19]

In the 1990s Koontz has a new project under way with CBS-TV: it plans to air "The Dean Koontz Theatre" sometime in the future. Included will be *Darkfall, Eyes of Darkness, The Face of Fear,* and *Night Chills.* There is no word on whether or not Koontz plans to write any more children's books such as *Oddkins,* which attracted an audience composed of all ages.

Dean Koontz seems content for now to be writing in cross-genre fields, and it appears that the public appreciates his present style. As a popular author, Koontz has clearly thought out his own philosophy of writing, the themes he wishes to develop, and the messages he wants to present. Since he writes in genres that include scenes of sex and violence, he has not shied from presenting them. He defends the use of violence in this way: "I *do* believe violence in a novel should have moral purpose. It should not be used merely to titillate, but to show that violence is only a last resort and that those who turn to it without compunction are sick. Most anti-violence types can't seem to distinguish between subtle issues of violence in a narrative and just plain pandering, and they are witlessly convinced that merely not reading or talking about such things will eliminate those problems from the world."[20]

4. The Eternal Struggle of Good and Evil: John Saul and Robert R. McCammon

One of the most common underlying themes in horror fiction is the struggle between good and evil. Good versus evil is a subject present in the mythology and legends of all cultures. In mythology the embodiments of good and evil are often superhuman gods. In horror literature evil is frequently portrayed as an occult force bent on revenge, power, mischief, and the corruption of human beings. In religion evil is usually visualized as a devil or demon. The side of good, however, is not always so clearly drawn, for the best that can be found to represent good in many legends and stories is the good to be found in people, an inner goodness that is often at odds with the darker aspects of human personalities. When individuals are forced to confront superhuman evil, or even pure evil in human form, the sides are usually uneven and the outcome is always in question.

Some people believe that evil is the ever-present opposite of good and that the one cannot exist without the other. Other people believe that evil exists in order to tempt mere mortals so as to test their courage and moral convictions. Whatever is involved, good and evil exist as elements in a never-ending struggle, in reality and in literature.

This struggle is usually present in one form or another in horror fiction. Because it is difficult to tell an exciting story without some kind of conflict and because the characters an author creates must be sympathetic to the reader, the side of good is often represented by human beings. Evil in a horror story may take the form of the ancient, evil beings alluded to in many legends and modern fiction; of an evil come to earth from another world; of scientific terrors unleashed by mad scientists; or even of psychological evil as evidenced in human beings of all ages.

Two best-selling writers of horror fiction have been particularly successful in portraying this eternal struggle between good and evil: John Saul and Robert R. McCammon.

John Saul: Is the Worst Horror Supernatural or Psychological?

I feel I give you a choice of interpretation. I always try to have three possible explanations going. There can be a supernatural or occult explanation, a psychological explanation, or else the murderer is just plain mad and getting even. If you dig the occult, you can say, "Aha, the ghost done it!"—or caused it to be done. If you believe in psychosis, you can say, "Hmmmm, she was crazy." If you think people are no damned good, you can say, "See? Another mean cop."[1]

—John Saul

John Saul grew up in Whittier, California, in what he has termed a relatively happy home. He decided at the age of 10 that he wanted to be a writer, and he describes himself at that age as a loner who read a lot. Later, as a student at Antioch College, he seriously considered becoming an archaeologist. Fortunately, however, at a lecture he met the eminent anthropologist Margaret Mead, who discouraged him from this career track by telling him such work is usually done in museums, rather than in the field, and can be boring for some.[2]

Chronology: John Saul's Life and Works

1942   John Woodruff Saul III born 25 February in Pasadena, California, the son of John W. Saul, Jr., an oil refinery worker, and Elizabeth Lee Saul.

1959–1965   Attends Antioch College, Cerritos College, Montana State University, and San Francisco State College.

1965–1977   Works in a variety of jobs, including selling real estate in Hawaii, renting cars, working in theater and in a drug rehabilitation program, and doing technical writing and general office work. Writes and sells some pornography under a pseudonym.

1973   Moves to Seattle.

1977   *Suffer the Children.*

1982   *The God Project,* first hardcover book.

Saul returned to his original ambition of becoming a writer, but his academic career suffered. After attending four colleges, he left school without a degree, in order to pursue his goal. He did not set out to be a horror writer; his early, still-unpublished novels were mostly comedy murder mysteries. During this period Saul also wrote some pornography, which was published under a pseudonym, and at times worked in the theater, trying his hand at drama.

John Saul earned his living doing all sorts of work in offices, real estate enterprises, and social agencies. By the time he had reached his thirties he was starting to feel discouraged about his chances for success in his chosen field. He was living in Seattle, working in a drug rehabilitation program, but was not yet ready to totally give up his dream.

At this point a New York agent, Jane Berkey, suggested Saul try his hand at horror fiction because of its popularity. After reading several horror books, Saul composed an outline, was granted a contract, and wrote the book in just 28 days; *Suffer the Children* was published shortly before his thirty-fifth birthday (Chambers and Blackman, 80).

On being asked in an interview if he was surprised by the book's instant success, Saul remarked,

> I should have been more surprised than I was, but both my agent and my editor had told me from the first moment they read the outline that it was going to be a bestseller. So when it actually became a bestseller we were not terribly surprised. Of course, we were all very young and very naive at the time. Since then we've learned we were very, very fortunate in that nothing went wrong with that whole project. The outline was right, the manuscript was right and delivered on time, and the publicity campaign was excellent and actually coincided with the release of the book. All of these things, of course, we've now realized don't always happen that way.[3]

Suffer the Children

Saul's first best-seller published in 1977 is the story of two sisters, Elizabeth and Sarah Conger. They live with their parents,

Jack and Rose, in the old Conger mansion overlooking the Maine seacoast. A hundred years earlier another Conger child, Beth, was cruelly attacked by her own father and killed; her father stuffed the broken body in a secret cave and then committed suicide. Now history has repeated itself, for Jack, in an an uncontrollable passion, has attacked Sarah, his younger child, in a scene witnessed by Elizabeth. Though Jack did not rape Sarah, the brutal beating has left her mute and disturbed, a student in a special school run by Dr. Charles Belter.

Sarah's parents have turned increasingly to their elder daughter, Elizabeth, now 13, to shoulder the responsibility of caring for Sarah. Elizabeth is blond, seemingly wise beyond her years, and incredibly patient with the irrational Sarah. Jack's attack on Sarah has obviously put great stress on the Congers' marriage, and they are grateful for Elizabeth's maturity in dealing with Sarah, since the old housekeeper is of little help.

The reader learns, however, that Elizabeth is not the balanced, rational girl she appears to her parents to be. Elizabeth, who looks very much like the portrait of the earlier Beth, is far more disturbed than her seemingly crazy sister, Sarah. Sarah knows to some degree what is going on, but because of her emotional state she cannot stop the terrible events from happening.

Elizabeth knows where the secret cave is, the cave that still contains the skeleton of long-dead Beth. She goes to the cave with the body of her dead cat and proceeds to set up a manic tea party with the cat's corpse and the skeleton as Sarah watches from the shadows. Not satisfied with her cast of characters, Elizabeth tricks a girlfriend, Kathy, into the cave and keeps her there, a prisoner. The terrified Kathy suffers at the hands of her psychotic keeper, but Sarah is able to get her some water. Elizabeth then traps another child, little Jimmy, for her tea parties, which seem to be psychodramas organized by the disturbed adolescent to act out her feelings and frustrations over her family situation. At her last tea party, Elizabeth articulates her problems as she forces her victims to play roles:

> "Now," she said. "Kathy, you're the mother. And Jimmy's the
> father. And Cecil [the dead cat] is your baby. Your crazy baby.
> Feed your baby, Mother."

Kathy sat quietly, barely able to keep herself upright.

"I said to feed your baby!" Elizabeth demanded. When Kathy still made no move toward the cat, Elizabeth raised her fist and brought it down hard on Kathy's back, driving her face first into the center of the table. "You do what I tell you," Elizabeth snarled through her teeth. . . .

Jimmy froze for a moment, then found his tongue.

"Nice baby," he said. "Here's some nice food for the nice baby."

"*Her name's Sarah!*" Elizabeth screamed. Don't you even know your baby's name? What kind of a father are you?" . . .

"She doesn't answer, does she?" Elizabeth said softly. Jimmy shook his head.

"Do you know why she doesn't answer?" Elizabeth asked smoothly.

Jimmy shook his head again.

"*Because she's crazy!*" Elizabeth screamed. . . .

"Then she's a bad child," Elizabeth said. "She's crazy and she's bad. Punish her." Jimmy didn't move. *Punish her!* . . .

"Don't touch her," Elizabeth commanded. "You don't like to touch Mother, do you? She wants you to touch her, but you don't like to. We know what you like, don't we?" She leered at the little boy, who stared at her in bewilderment.

"You like the baby, don't you? We know you like the baby better than you like Mother, don't we?" And suddenly her voice rose, and the cavern was filled to overflowing with the sound of her words.[4]

Elizabeth becomes increasingly agitated by the portrait of the earlier, murdered Beth that hangs over the mantel, and the legend of the family's sordid history hangs heavily over all. Everywhere is a sense of doom and foreboding.

Another victim, Jeff, is persuaded to come to the cave with Elizabeth, who then goes beserk, killing and dismembering her prisoners. She returns home, cleans herself up, and apparently blocks out the memory of her deeds, as she has done previously. But shortly thereafter Sarah is seen by the family, walking home from the cave, dragging a child's arm with her. It is decided that Sarah must be institutionalized, and as the bodies are not found, no explanations are forthcoming at this point for the police chief, who cannot locate the missing children.

The short, final section of *Suffer the Children* takes place 15

years later. We learn that Sarah has almost recovered and is
being released under certain conditions for a limited time to go
home with her sister, Elizabeth. Jack and Rose Conger have died
in a boating accident, probably suicide, and the two sisters are all
that is left of the Conger family. Sarah has remembered some of
the trauma of her youth but cannot bring forth the memory of
that terrible day when she hauled the arm home. Elizabeth seems
placid and normal, living peacefully in the old house.

The old police chief arrives to tell the sisters that the cave has
been discovered, along with the skeletal remains of the missing
children. There is talk of bringing Sarah to trial, now that there
is definite proof of death. When Sarah is told of the discovery her
memory of that awful day returns. Her mind snaps again, this
time forever, as she screams, "Elizabeth— . . . Elizabeth . . . *Eliza
. . . beth. Beth! Beth!*"

Sarah returns to the sanatorium. Elizabeth goes to the attic,
an old family attic where all relics are saved. She finds the portrait of Beth, stares at it, and then returns it to its old place above
the mantel. She also discovers Beth's diary and reads the earlier
child's account of her growing uneasiness about her father's interest in her. Some truth of the whole story dawns on Elizabeth.
She finds a kitchen knife and, taking her old cat with her, walks
toward the location of the old cave. Here the text ends with these
words:

> As she walked through the night, the odd inscription in the
> diary ran through her mind over and over:
>   *Suffer the Children*, it had read, *to Come Unto Me.*
> Elizabeth Conger was answering the summons. (*Suffer*, 378)

This ambiguous ending leaves many uncertainties and shivers
in the reader's mind. What will happen next? Will Elizabeth kill
the cat and set off another chain of horror? Or will she do something else? And if she does, what? What a delicious thing to spec-
ulate about when lying awake in bed at night.

Suffer the Children capitalizes on a popular theme, the child as
villain and victim. In modern literature the best-known child villain is the one portrayed in Maxwell Anderson's play *The Bad*

Seed. In this play and in its later, successful movie version the viewer finds fascination growing as it becomes increasingly clear that the almost-perfect little blond girl (played by Patty Mc-Cormack in the movie) is a psychological monster capable of murder to get her own way. Saul's Elizabeth in *Suffer the Children* would seem to be copied from *The Bad Seed.* The success of the play and film in the secure Eisenhower years gave no clues, however, of the curious phenomenon that emerged in the late 1970s of audience delight in rotten kids.

Amitai Etzione, a noted sociologist, commented on this popularity by tying it to a general sociological condition in which parents seemed to be unhappy with their less-than-perfect children and, as a result, an antichild feeling was evident in the country.[5] John Saul did not intend deep interpretations of the evil child; rather, he views his role as that of entertainer. He finds he is successful at this and enjoys writing psychological horror thrillers: "That's basically my approach. I simply take a setting that I know, put certain pieces together and try to write a good yarn. I don't *believe* any of it. I know it's tempting to look for parallels, but I've always believed that you must separate artists from their work. I mean, you can read anything you want into fiction. I've heard people analyze *Suffer the Children,* trying to get some significance from the fact that Jack Conger has the same initials as Jesus Christ. They're convinced that I'm after some deep message—and I'm not" (Kramer, 18).

Saul's many unsuccessful years as an unpublished novelist have resulted in crisp, precise prose and careful plotting in even his earliest published books. Critics in the horror field, however, have expressed with dismay some feeling that his use of children as villains and victims is too calculating and cynical. Said one critic, "For each new horror novel that portrayed young characters with conscience, a dozen appeared in which teenagers, children, and even infants were imbued with evil for no apparent reason other than their age and, of course, exploitable innocence. One of the worst offenders was, intriguingly, one of the field's major sellers—John Saul, whose aptly titled first novel, *Suffer the Children* (1977), says it all."[6]

Another critic and horror writer, Charles L. Grant, comments:

> With few exceptions, those who constitute the American book-buying public (and most of these are women) have a special affection for children. I suspect it's either because they've forgotten what it's like to be a child, or because the Romantic in them insists that children are innately White (good, innocent, unstained) and should be saved at all costs—if for no other reason than that they represent the future.
>
> To cast them in roles which we do not ordinarily ascribe to them is a calculated marketing/writing device. Because they are (from the popular Romantic viewpoint) the innocents, they become all the more terrifying when they are discovered to be prime agents of the Dark. After all, who would suspect a helpless blind girlchild of wanting to return from the dead (after being shoved off a cliff) to destroy a family and a seacoast town (*Comes the Blind Fury*), or a rosy-cheeked little shaver who has an ambassador for a father and a curious black dog for a guardian (*The Omen*)?[7]

Stephen King offers helpful comments regarding the use of children as villains:

> Children are rarely cruel on purpose, and they even more rarely torture, as they understand the concept; they may however kill in the spirit of experimentation, watching the death struggles of the bug on the sidewalk in the same clinical way that a biologist would watch a guinea pig die after inhaling a whiff of nerve gas.
>
> Now, don't get me wrong or misinterpret what I'm saying. Kids can be mean and unlovely, and when you see them at their worst, they can make you think black thoughts about the future of the human race. But meanness and cruelty, although related, are not the same thing at all. A cruel action is a studied action; it requires a bit of thought. Meanness, on the other hand, is unpremeditated and unthinking. The results may be similar for the person—usually another child—who gets the butt end, but it seems to me that in a moral society, intent or lack of it is pretty important.[8]

Saul himself does not respond vehemently to such comments. In fact, he admits that the first book, *Suffer the Children,* was gruesome and rough, so much so that he views the death scenes as so disgusting he can't read them (Kramer, 18).

More Tortured Children

Since his success with *Suffer the Children* Saul has published about one book a year. His early books were all published as original paperbacks, and the first five all used the theme of hapless children and youthful avenging figures. Saul did tone down his descriptions of violence in these books; nonetheless, that action did not discourage his growing number of fans.

Saul's second novel, *Punish the Sinners* (1978), upset some readers in another way, however. In *Punish the Sinners* Saul tells the story of a teacher, Peter Balsam, who finds his pupils at St. Francis Xavier High School overcome with a sort of mass hysteria, resulting in suicide attempts. A former seminary student, Peter is seeking meaning for his life and is attracted to the Society of St. Peter Martyr. The society, however, is not calculated to strengthen faith in conventional ways, and Peter is also troubled by the ominous atmosphere of the church and school. Is it possible that the spirits of medieval, malevolent priests from the Inquisition are in Neilsville? In the end Peter dies without solving the school's problems or stopping the disturbed Monsignor Vernon from his path of evil.

In telling about the controversy regarding the book, Saul says, "After *Punish the Sinners* was written, I got a great deal of flack from Catholics for my portrayal of the priests in Neilsville. I also got a letter from someone in Portland, Oregon, who wanted to know whether I was talking about a particular priest in Washington. Turned out there is a town out there that looks exactly like Neilsville, complete with the Catholic school on the hill and a strange priest who had all of these terribly fourteenth-century ideas that he was trying to inflict on the town" (Kramer, 17).

The next three books, *Cry for the Strangers* (1979), *Comes the Blind Fury* (1980), and *When the Wind Blows* (1981), continued Saul's writing themes of small towns with big troubles, mysterious and evil legends from the past, and children without sunny, happy days. Saul's skill as a writer was noted by a few critics, who made such comments as, "An accomplished fashioner of the simple horror story, Saul combines sympathetic and skillful characterization with evocative use of atmosphere to create a well-crafted, although predictable, chiller."[9]

Later Books

By his fifth horror novel Saul's publishers felt he was ready to be published in hardcover, and *The God Project* came out in that format in 1982. Although not as successful as his earlier books, *The God Project* was Saul's first attempt to blend in scientific, technological horrors. This idea of science being used for evil is also picked up in the later *Brain Child* (1985) and *Creature* (1989).

Creature demonstrates as well Saul's return to more descriptive violence, as does *The Unloved,* published a year earlier. Saul explains that less violence "seemed to work fine up until *The Unloved.* Then I realized I hadn't done a real blood bath for a while and I thought it was about time. And I have to admit I had an awful lot of fun with old Marguerite" (Kisner, 6).

In *Creature* Saul sets his story in a small Colorado company town, and typical of many small towns, the folks who live there are very supportive of the high school football team. Dr. Martin Ames, hired by TarrenTech to run the sports center, takes Mark Tanner, a weak and shy newcomer, through his improvement program, transforming Mark into a strong athlete. But as in such tales as H. G. Wells's *The Island of Dr. Moreau,* these experiments don't always work and Mark becomes uncontrollable, a town terror rather than a town hero. Yet Mark is not a complete monster, for some of his gentle feelings break through on occasion. In the end the reader finds Mark still alive, living alone in the mountains, but maintaining a furtive relationship with his sister. Mark has become a classic tragic beast, one to be pitied rather than feared.

When asked how he got the idea for the novel, Saul responded:

> I know *exactly* where I got the idea. I was watching the evening
> news about a year and a half ago, and there was a report on
> human growth hormones. The report got to talking in the fu-
> ture about "designer bodies." That there will come a time when
> you can pick your body style and there will be a combination of
> hormones that will allow you to have that body style. And I
> thought, *"That's* kind of creepy!" Two minutes later I thought,
> "There's the idea for the next book. How is this all going to
> work?" Immediately I saw one of those small towns where the
> major focus of everything is the high school football team, and
> what if one of these little towns figured out a way to make their
> team absolutely unbeatable? Bingo![10]

Teenage readers have reacted favorably to *Creature,* as they
have to Saul's earlier books. Saul, at first somewhat surprised by
this popularity, explains:

> I have a thirteen-year-old niece, and my sister wouldn't let her
> read my books. "Uncle John writes trash, and you're not going
> to read it." Well, my niece went off to camp last summer and
> the camp director was reading *Comes the Blind Fury,* and Al-
> lison said, "My Uncle John wrote that book," and the director
> said, "Oh, really? I suppose you read this one already." Allison
> said, "No, I'm not allowed to read Uncle John's books," and the
> director said, "Well, that's ridiculous. They're pretty good,
> they're great fun. Read."
> So my niece read *Comes the Blind Fury,* and when she came
> home she told her mother she wanted to read the rest of them.
> She's a big fan of mine now. Much of the fan mail is from teen-
> aged girls like Allison. They all want to know when one of my
> books is going to be made into a movie, and has the part of the
> villain been cast yet. They all want to play Elizabeth (*Suffer
> the Children*). They want to be Michelle (*Blind Fury*).
> (Kramer, 18)

John Saul maintains a business office in Seattle and does his
writing there. He is often able to write his best-sellers quickly,
once the original idea and outline are developed. He sometimes
obtains psychological details from his roommate, Michael Sack, a

Chronology: Robert R. McCammon's Life and Works

1952   Born 17 July in Birmingham, Alabama, the elder of the two sons of Jack McCammon, a musician, and Barbara Bundy McCammon, an aspiring actress. Reared by his grandparents.

1975   Graduates from the University of Alabama with a major in journalism. Works at a variety of jobs.

1978   First book, *Baal*.

1981   Marries Sally Sanders, an elementary school teacher.

1983   First hardcover book, *Mystery Walk*.

1984   Conceives the idea of a new association, Horror Writers of America.

1985   First best-seller, *Swan Song*.

clinical psychologist. When an interviewer asked Saul a question about providing closing messages for readers, he responded, "I don't think I have any. I don't have any messages for anybody. I'm primarily an entertainer. As long as I'm giving people a good read, I'm happy" (Kisner, 6).

Robert R. McCammon: Has Dark Fantasy Gone As Far As It Can?

> Yes, horror writing is certainly a positive force. I think it's like a smart little bad-ass in a church full of stiff-backed conservatives, and the preacher is emoting up a storm and on a roll, but everytime he shouts "Amen!" in sweating fervor, the kid shouts, "Why?" Horror fiction upsets apple carts, burns old buildings and stampedes the horses; it questions and yearns for answers, and it takes nothing for granted. It's not safe, and it probably rots your teeth, too. Horror fiction can be a guide through a nightmare world, entered freely and by the reader's own will. And since horror can be many, many things and go in many, many directions, that guided nightmare ride can shock, educate, illuminate, threaten, shriek, and whisper before it lets the readers loose. It's always new, always creating itself over and over again, trying to attain an impossible perfection. I love it![11]
>
> —Robert R. McCammon

Robert "Rick" McCammon was born and reared in Birmingham, Alabama. His father, a musician who played with dance bands, evidently left when Rick was still young. His mother was trying to establish herself as an actress in Hollywood, and so Rick and his younger brother, Michael, were essentially brought up by their grandparents. His grandfather, a wealthy Birmingham businessman, had a cold personality and a stark, fundamentalist moral code, but McCammon remembers that the older man may have been responsible in part for making him a writer: "But for all that, my grandfather did do two wonderful things: he read to me, and he told me ghost stories. He unlocked my mind, which helped me escape the realities of being a skinny, gawky, painfully shy kid. I started reading everything I could lay my hands on" (Landsdale, 25).

McCammon attended the University of Alabama, receiving his degree with a major in journalism in 1975. He was unable to find a job as a reporter, however, and tried a variety of undesired occupations, including working in a B. Dalton bookstore (where he met his moonlighting wife-to-be), ushering in a theater, writing advertising copy, and editing newspaper copy.

This was a frustrating period for the young McCammon. He had truly wanted to be a journalist. Although he had written a few short stories when he was younger, he hadn't really considered a career as a novelist. Writing was a sort of hobby. Yet during this time McCammon decided to write a novel, expanding on an idea he had had while still in college. Writing that book became a form of escapism for McCammon, one that eventually transformed itself from escape hatch to full-time writing career. Charles de Lint, writing in *Horrorstruck,* tells us that McCammon "wrote *Baal* at night after work and found himself *'running* to get home to work on it. No novel I've done since has come together so smoothly. It just seemed to leap onto the pages, and thank God, it took me out of a very bad situation and kept me going.'"[12]

It is unusual for an author to have a first novel quickly accepted and published. The event, while important to McCammon, was a mixed blessing, for he was still learning his craft as a writer: "I was a kid when I wrote *Baal* in 1977, just two years out of college. . . . I was blocked and frustrated and full of rage, and that's what spilled out and became *Baal.* That book is all anger and shouting. I've learned that sometimes a whisper communicates more effectively. I've learned about tones and undercurrents and foreshadowing and that characters—real people—rarely have souls that are all black and white. I think I've learned compassion for my characters, and I hope that shows through my work" (Landsdale, 25).

McCammon admits that his early works were immature. Unlike John Saul, whose long apprenticeship of writing before publication provided an opportunity to sharpen his skills, Mc-

Cammon did his learning in a more public arena: "*Baal, Bethany's Sin,* and *Nightboat* probably should've stayed locked away in my desk drawer and never shown the light of day, much less publication. They're feeble attempts, but I believe in what a friend told me a long time ago, 'You do the best you can at the time.' At that time, those books were the best I could do. I was learning and I was lucky. . . . I was allowed by the vagaries of the publishing business to break in probably before I was really ready. It's amazing to me that those books still sell" (Landsdale, 25).

McCammon continued to write, and his second novel, *Bethany's Sin,* appeared two years after *Baal,* in 1980, and was followed by his third book later that same year, *The Night Boat. Bethany's Sin,* like *Baal,* was a traditional horror story. All deal with supernatural themes: in *Baal* the title character is a monster that can be stopped only by superhuman means; in *Bethany's Sin* a peaceful town is disrupted by the spirit of an ancient Amazonian cult bent on eliminating the male population of Bethany's Sin, Pennsylvania. The next of these early efforts, the *Night Boat,* deals with a Nazi ghost ship that lurks in an oceanic abyss. The shipwrecked U-boat is discovered:

> Kip listened. No sounds, no movement. He couldn't stop shaking; his body was out of control. "They're dead. . . ." he spat out finally. "They're DEAD!"
> And then the echo, coming up around them, engulfing them with a word that seemed strange and terrible.
> And untrue.[13]

After the publication of *Bethany's Sin,* McCammon turned to writing full-time. He quit his job and married Sally Sanders, an elementary school teacher, in 1981. His next book, *They Thirst,* was longer than his earlier works and used a popular horror theme, vampires. This particular jolly band is lurking about in Los Angeles. In an afterword to the reprint edition of 1988, McCammon explains:

> *They Thirst* began, actually, as a novel called *The Hungry.* It was set in Chicago, and involved a gang of vampiric teenagers.

I got about two hundred pages into it before I began to feel constricted. When you get that feeling, you know things aren't going right. You have to put aside the manuscript and think about it, and let me tell you that deciding to cast away two hundred pages of a manuscript and start over again from scratch is the kind of decision that makes cold sweat break out on your skin.

I wanted a vampire novel with a huge cast, set in a city where anything was possible. Ah, Los Angeles. The City of Angels. Eternal Youth Shall Reign Forever, Amen. . . .

I think a Vampire King would find Los Angeles a wonderland. He would know that such a beautiful beast has a huge dark belly. And in that darkness, surrounded by pallid forms who fall at his feet in worship, even a Vampire King might become a star.[14]

These early books by McCammon were not reviewed in a particularly positive light. But they were selling well, and McCammon switched publishers, from Avon to a house that promised hardcover publications, Holt, Rinehart and Winston. *Mystery Walk,* published in 1983, and *Usher's Passing,* published in 1984, marked not only McCammon's break into the hardcover market but also his maturation as an author. Both books received a number of good reviews, although the publisher did not promote the books very well.[15] These titles also showed his development as a distinctive horror writer. McCammon's earlier works were often compared with the books of Stephen King, with the idea that McCammon was imitating King, as shown in this comment by Douglas E. Winter, reviewing 1981 publications: "Inevitably, we were treated to a retelling of the modern classic vampire novel, Stephen King's *'Salem's Lot* (1975), in the form of Robert R. McCammon's *They Thirst* (Avon, 1981), which uses Los Angeles as an up-scaled version of King's small Maine town and threw in elements of *The Stand* as well. As in his earlier novels, McCammon's prose was animated and his intent apparently sincere, but *They Thirst* reflected a paucity of original ideas, seemingly content to echo recently successful works of other writers."[16]

McCammon explains:

It was difficult for me because my first novel *was* published, and in a sense I learned to write in public. I was searching for my own style of expression, my own voice in public. I think that's where the idea that I was overly influenced by King comes from.

It was probably true, because I was reading a lot of Stephen King, and even though I was reading a lot of other people too I thought this guy was top of the form! This is the person who has led all the others—so I think that's where a lot of the early criticism came from.[17]

The More Mature Works

Mystery Walk is a traditional horror story with supernatural elements. Although it can be considered one of McCammon's more mature works, it can also be regarded as a return-to-roots book, for it is the first of his novels to be set in the Southeast. This book is the one McCammon says is his own favorite to date,[18] and the Literary Guild chose *Mystery Walk* as one of its selections.

Mystery Walk begins as a story of conflict between Billy Creekmore, a boy who is able to help earthbound spirits find release and whose mother is suspected of witchcraft, and Wayne Falconer, a young faith healer and the son of an evangelist preacher. Although these two sympathetic characters seem at first to be in opposition to each other, it later becomes evident that both represent good in a struggle against the evil Shape Changer, a primeval bestial entity that gains strength from the fear of human beings. In an eerie climax the three meet in the stark Mexican desert, and good confronts evil in a fatal battle. In the end only Billy survives.

Usher's Passing poses the question, What if all the Ushers didn't die with the fall of their house in Edgar Allan Poe's famous story? Rix Usher is the modern descendant of the Ushers, heir to the family's munitions fortune and its huge, sinister estate, which includes a moldering mansion and a specter known as the Pumpkin Man. McCammon admits that the character of Rix Usher is somewhat autobiographical; his own wealthy grandfather, for example, had wanted him to go into the family business, much as Rix Usher considers doing in *Usher's Passing*.

Like McCammon, Rix Usher is portrayed as a horror writer. McCammon's own childhood home, although large, could hardly have been comparable to the approach to Usherlands, however, as shown in McCammon's very Gothic description:

> Rix suddenly felt the back of his neck prickle. If he'd been look-ing at a map of property lines, he wouldn't have known with any greater certainty that they had entered Usher domain. The forest seemed darker, the autumn leaves of such deep reds and purples that they appeared to shimmer with an oily blackness. The black canopy of leaves overhung the road, and tangles of briars—the kind that could gash to the bone and snap off—twisted in ugly corkscrews as dangerous as barbed wire. Mas-sive scabs of stone clung to the hillsides, threatening to slide down and smash the limo into junk. Rix realized his palms were sweating. The wilderness seemed to be a hostile environ-ment unsuited for a civilized human being—yet this was the land that Hudson Usher had fallen in love with. Or, perhaps, seen as a challenge to be broken. In any case, it had never been Rix's cup of thorns.[19]

Rix has already inherited part of the Usher "fortune," including extreme sensitivity to noise, a tendency toward insanity, and fam-ily curses. On top of all this Rix feels heavy guilt about the fam-ily's armaments business, gaining wealth from making the machines that cause human misery and destruction. Though Rix seems to be a weak symbol of good for this McCammon novel, he does manage to make the morally right decision in the end. Yet as in all good horror stories, evil is never fully vanquished, for one cannot be certain the dreadful Pumpkin Man has truly been destroyed.

Generally good critical acclaim was accorded *Usher's Passing*. One of the these commentaries appeared in *Rave Reviews*, stat-ing: "McCammon must have read Poe's classic dozens of times—every small allusion to the family is expanded and explored in the sequel. The novel is convincing and frightening, and even explains the curious disease that wastes each descendant of the Usher line."[20]

The Best-Sellers

Swan Song

In 1987 *Swan Song,* Rick McCammon's longest book to date, was published. A genre crossover novel, it is a doomsday book in which a nuclear holocaust is visited on the world. In the ensuing desolation a few survivors try to make it in this grim, futuristic society, but evil in the form of an ancient malevolence is intent on destroying the child, Swan, for he is the hope of a decent future for humankind.

Swan Song was a landmark book for McCammon, for it was his first best-seller and his first publication with Pocket Books. In addition to giving the book a generous amount of publicity, Mc-Cammon's new publisher solicited quotations from established horror writers to use on the cover of the original paperback. McCammon feels these endorsements from Dean R. Koontz and John Saul were valuable in creating more sales for the book. Moreover, the effort also helped assure him of the pointlessness of insisting on hardcover publication of books when paperbacks reach more people: "I realized that I was more concerned that my books be read than by the form in which they came out. That's why I am very happy at Pocket. They have given my books wide publication and they helped me find a whole new audience" (Adler, 123).

With its use of both horror and science fiction, as well as the apocalyptic theme, *Swan Song* is sometimes compared with Stephen King's *The Stand*. At this point in McCammon's writing career, however, the comparisons with King are more favorable than before, as shown in this review in *School Library Journal* "Apocalyptic fiction abounds, but *Swan Song,* epic in its proportion and scope, is as strong as Stephen King's *The Stand* (Doubleday, 1978). Unlike King's view of the post World War III world, which focused on a Satan-like figure of immense power, *Swan Song* is realistic, with good and evil coming from the human condition.[21]

Indeed, most of the reviewers of this work comment on the struggle between good and evil. One, Eddy C. Bertin, describes *Swan Song* as "a rollercoaster ride into a world of terror and horror, but also of wonder and beauty, a story which is cruel and compassionate, a novel of eternal struggle, and eternal hope.[22]

Stinger

McCammon followed the success of *Swan Song* with another best-seller, *Stinger* (1988), more clearly a science fiction/horror novel. Set in a bleak Texas town, *Stinger* describes the battle between opposing alien forces that possess the bodies of earthlings. In talking about this book, McCammon says:

> I chose the Texas desert as a setting because it's such a harsh, empty environment. There is simply nothing there for individuals to react to—there is nothing but other people, nothing to hide behind. The characters must face themselves. They had to grow, or perish. . . .
>
> I guess you could say my stories are about what characters do when faced with "The Wall." When an individual comes face to face with *the* crisis of their life—The Wall—they either go up or down. Many of my characters become bigger than they were, they grow. I try to offer my readers something more than entertainment. I give them a positive experience, a sort of reward. I want the reader to feel good about himself when he closes the book.[23]

The Wolf's Hour, Blue World, and Mine

McCammon's next published work, *The Wolf's Hour* (1987), is set in the past, rather than the futuristic world of science fiction. Michael Gallatin is a werewolf, and British intelligence authorities in the desperate days of World War II use Gallatin as secret agent. One critic declared:

> *The Wolf's Hour* is a taut historical novel, . . . without an ounce
> of fat or a wasted word. The action moves at compelling speed
> . . . in two merging plotlines with a cinematic elegance rarely
> found in genre novels. . . .
>   McCammon . . . breathes vitality into every character and
> scene. After *The Wolf's Hour,* werewolf stories can never be the
> same.[24]

Blue World (1989) was another departure for McCammon, for it is a collection of short stories, most published previously. Interestingly, the collection was first published in Great Britain, showing the growth of McCammon's international reputation as an author. Reviewer Patrick Jones offers this reaction to the stories: "Each story is packed with lasting images; it's not a blue world but one of bright colors, falling shadows, and blood red murders. McCammon works his magic in genres like science fiction, horror, mystery, and suspense thriller. A work on par with King's *Night Shift* that should appeal to the same audience."[25]

McCammon's most recent published work, *Mine* (1990), is a suspense thriller without the supernatural elements of traditional dark fantasy. Mary Terrel, known as Mary Terror in her days with the terrorist group Storm Front, steals a baby to gain reentry to her resurrected group. The baby's mother, Laura Clayborne, pursues Mary across the country in a desperate journey to get her baby back. Here McCammon again shows his skill in portraying personifications of good and evil. As one reviewer observed, "McCammon does an admirable job of showing a disturbed mind going right off the edge with Mary Terror, but more interestingly, perhaps, is how he cuts to the heart of a mother's protective urges to show us just how far a woman might go to reclaim what is hers."[26]

McCammon the Writer

Interviewers often describe McCammon as a perfect southern gentleman: handsome, soft-spoken, and charming. He appears to be refreshingly candid in his interviews, and he obviously enjoys his writing career. His own beliefs come through in his writing, for plainly he believes people are basically good: "Horror fiction must be more than scares. Yes, it's great to create a good scare, and that can be difficult enough in itself; but the best of horror fiction is about human experience. Maybe it's a kinked view of humanity, and maybe gore splatters the pages here and there, but that's because we're horror writers and it leaks out of our pens on its own. The best of horror fiction is not that bag of bones I spoke about earlier; it's a whole body, complete with beating heart and questing, introspective mind."[27]

5. Monsters, Vampires, and Werewolves: The Sympathetic Beasts of Anne Rice and Chelsea Quinn Yarbro

One of the most familiar villains in horror books and movies is the monster. The monster is an easily recognizable fear for most of us; the monster is the bogeyman of childhood who hides under the bed and lurks just outside the window in the dark. The monster's "gonna get ya if ya don't watch out."

The monster is present in every society and culture. The monster may be a godlike mythological figure or a mysterious furry beast that rules in the forest. The monster in more modern civilizations may be present as the evolutional freak of science fiction tales or as the result of nuclear testing. Most recently, the monster has been created from ecological carelessness, as in the case of the Toxic Avenger.

Monsters not only prey on weak human beings but are sometimes able to make human beings like themselves. Vampires beget new vampires; werewolves get recruits; zombies find new buddies. These victims also infect humans creating even more monsters. The crux of the ancient fear of supernatural monsters is simple: losing one's life to a terrible beast is bad, but losing one's soul to such a creature is even worse.

Although many kinds of monsters have inhabited the pages of horror literature, there are, according to James B. Twitchell, only three major types that have endured in modern horror fiction: vampires, as exemplified by Dracula; man-made, Frankenstein's monster kinds of creations; and variations of Jekyll/Hyde and the wolfman, the last being the bestial side that exists in all human beings.[1] Twitchell explains in his introduction to *Dreadful Pleasures*, "Like fairy tales that prepare the child for the anxieties of separation, modern horror myths prepare the teenager for the anxieties of reproduction. They are fantastic, ludicrous, crude, and important distortions of real life situations, not in the service of repression (though they certainly have that temporary effect), but of instruction. These fever dreams do more than make us shiver; they are fables of sexual identity. Horror myths establish social patterns not of escape, but entry. Night visitors prepare us for daylight" (Twitchell, 7).

In modern horror literature there have been stories about monsters, and many authors have enjoyed writing about the exploits of inhuman predators. But not all authors have been unsympathetic to these sorry creatures who cannot help being what they are. Two authors who have used "monsters" as their protagonists are Anne Rice and Chelsea Quinn Yarbro, both of whom force the reader to consider monsters in a somewhat different light. Such creatures usually don't want to be monsters, and their tortured souls ask for understanding from the reader.

Anne Rice: Who Is the Real Misfit?

To me the vampire is a powerful metaphor out of the deep imagination, with echoes of vegetation gods, blood sacrifice, thousands of images that are more dreamed of than spoken. These things evoke in people profoundly complex responses that are very hard to analyze. The vampire is a perfect metaphor for people who drain us dry, for our fear of the dead coming back, for the outsider who is in the midst of everything and

Chronology: Anne Rice's Life and Works

1941 Born 4 October in New Orleans, the daughter of Howard and Katherine Allen O'Brien.

1959–1960 Attends Texas Woman's University.

1961 Marries Stan Rice, a poet. They later have two children, Michelle (who in 1972 dies from leukemia), and Christopher, born in 1978.

1964 Receives B.A. from San Francisco State College (now University).

1971 Receives M.A. from San Francisco State College.

1976 *Interview with the Vampire,* first of a trilogy.

1989 Returns to New Orleans to live in her birthplace. *The Mummy.*

1990 *The Witching Hour.*

yet feels monstrous and completely cut off. And I think most
people feel that way at heart.[2]

—Anne Rice

Anne Rice was born into an Irish-American family in New Orleans, one of the most historic and exotic cities in America. The
French and Spanish background of the city, as well as Rice's own
ethnic background and interest in English literature, gave the
writer a strongly European outlook. In addition, the southern
Gothic atmosphere of the region has helped give Rice a fondness
for writing about eccentrics and outsiders, those who seem not to
belong to mainstream society.

As a child Rice loved to read, and she continued this love as a
teenager and adult. She comments about an early memory,
"When I was a child, we used to talk about books a lot in my
house. There was a story from the library going around in my
family called 'The White Silk Dress.' It was told from the point of
view of a child vampire. I never forgot that. I remember loving
the idea of a vampire in the first person telling the story, and I
also wanted to get into the vampire."[3]

Rice and her three sisters were reared in a strongly Catholic
home by their mother and their father, a sculptor. Through most
of her formative years Rice accompanied her grandmother to
church daily. She also attended Catholic parochial school. Today
she no longer practices the religion of her youth.

Creativity was stressed in Rice's childhood home,[4] and she
started writing early. As a young woman she married Stan Rice,
a poet, and they moved to San Francisco, a particularly exciting
city to live in during the 1960s, when the sexual revolution and
the birth of "flower power" was taking place. Yet she felt she
never really belonged in California. Her writing focused on bizarre things, historic settings, and exotic places. She says, "I was
writing stories that had nothing to do with reality. That's what I
felt comfortable writing about."[5]

In her prepublication days in San Francisco Rice concentrated
on rearing her daughter, Michele, and worked at a variety of jobs,
including cook, waitress, and insurance claims examiner. Michele's death in 1972 from leukemia, however, turned Rice in her

grief to finishing her first novel, which was about a vampire. Although rejected by a number of publishers, the book was finally bought and published by Knopf. *Interview with the Vampire* became a best-seller, and Anne Rice's career as an author was launched.

Vampire literature has been around for nearly two centuries, probably being born the same night as *Frankenstein,* when Mary and Percy Shelley, Lord Byron, and John Polidari told one another spooky stories on a stormy night in Switzerland. Byron's fragment of a story of a vampire was later completed and published by Polidari. It was at the end of the nineteenth century, however, that Bram Stoker's *Dracula* truly solidified the popularity of the vampire as a character in the Gothic horror tradition. Books, stories, plays, and movies about vampires have abounded ever since, including such modern classics as *I Am Legend,* by Richard Matheson, and *Hunger,* by Whitley Strieber. Anne Rice's vampire story was different, though, because it treated vampires as sympathetic creatures, outsiders who nonetheless had feelings and other human qualities. These vampires asked the reader to understand them.

The success of the image of the vampire as a sympathetic character has resulted in additional books about vampires by Rice, including *The Vampire Lestat* and *Queen of the Damned.* But she has not written these books in a direct sequence, for she has been involved in writing historical fiction and soft pornography as well. The latter, written under the pseudonyms Anne Rampling and A. N. Roquelaure, was done to fill the void Rice felt when she looked for the kind of pornography she herself wanted to read. Although she used pseudonyms for her erotica, Rice does not apologize for these books, feeling that pornography is completely worthwhile, a viewpoint referred to in most of her interviews.

Before the two sequels to *Interview with the Vampire* were published, Rice wrote two historical novels. One, *The Feast of All Saints,* deals with the subculture of the *gens de couleur libre* (free people of color) of New Orleans before the Civil War. Here Rice again deals with the theme of outsiders, as she tells the story of a mulatto brother and sister in a rigidly stratified society.

The other historical novel Rice wrote at this time was *Cry to*

Heaven, published in 1982. This book also tells the story of outsiders, this time the castrati of eighteenth-century Italy. The castrati were castrated boys trained to be singers, mutilated in order to save their voices from changing with manhood. Adored as singers, the castrati were usually viewed as freaks or—as the young hero views himself—with self-hatred, a "monster." Although Tonio, the novel's hero, reconciles himself to his fate enough that he is determined to be a great singer, he is also determined to avenge himself on his father, who arranged for his castration. Hence we have a story that, though strictly speaking is not a horror novel, parallels the plot of many monster books and films by having the poor creature seek revenge on the mad scientist (or whoever it was) who made him a monster in the first place.

Although most of us flee from monsters, it has been suggested that "Anne Rice did the opposite. She not only approached her monsters, but merged herself with them by casting them as central characters in fiction. 'I just get into their skin and everything happens.' Her reconstructed monsters take the form of social outcasts—vampires, witches, mummies, castrated opera singers and sexual outsiders—people who are excluded from participating in 'normal' society because of some personal condition deemed to be an offensive defect" (Ramsland, January 1990, 43).

In 1985 *The Vampire Lestat* appeared, followed by *Queen of the Damned* in 1988. After these two vampire books *The Mummy* was published. Anne Rice is still writing vampire books, and it is for them that she is most popular.

The Vampire Chronicles

Interview with the Vampire

Officially dubbed the Vampire Chronicles, Rice's vampire series began with the book *Interview with the Vampire.*

The premise of this novel is simple. A young reporter in San Francisco meets a man, Louis, who tells the incredulous boy that he, Louis, is a vampire. He tells his life story, which covers a span of 200 years.

Louis has spent his early years as a normal human being in Louisiana. A member of the privileged upper-class plantation society, Louis is 25 years old in 1791. Then he meets Lestat, an evil yet fascinating vampire who drafts him into vampiric membership and even shares his coffin with him. Louis discovers that much of vampire folklore, such as the repellent power of garlic and crosses, is nonsense. He also learns that vampires can, if necessary, survive on animal blood.

Louis does not love his mentor, Lestat, but is dependent on him at first to learn how to live as a vampire. Early in his new existence Louis yearns to find other vampires. He is unwilling to exist without others like himself, and he refuses to settle for the companionship of only Lestat.

Louis and Lestat wander through a New Orleans beset with fever and plague and acquire a five-year-old girl named Claudia, whom they initiate into their vampire clan. Although still a child, Claudia possesses great sensual attraction, and her new vampire parents outfit her in exquisite clothes to accentuate her beauty. Claudia is their pupil, and her mind expands rapidly, yet she is trapped forever in her child's body. Louis explains to the boy recording his story, "But her mind. It was a vampire's mind. And I strained to know how she moved towards womanhood. She came to talk more, though she was never other than a reflective person and could listen to me patiently by the hour without interruption. Yet more and more her doll-like face seemed to possess two totally aware adult eyes, and innocence seemed lost somewhere with neglected toys and the loss of a certain patience."[6]

Claudia is not happy with her vampire existence and is angry at being trapped forever in a child's body. She demands to know which of the two vampires, Louis or Lestat, has actually made her what she has become, a child vampire. On learning it was Lestat, Claudia vents great hatred on him. Finally she attempts to kill Lestat; Louis and Claudia, believing she has been successful, then leave for Europe to find others of their kind.

They travel first to the fabled homeland of vampires, Transylvania. In the Carpathians they find only mindless corpses, ghouls, not the vampire companions they are seeking. From there

Louis and Claudia go to Paris, where they discover Theatre des Vampires, in which real vampires perform their blood-draining acts for a jaded Parisian society. Louis and Claudia's fascination with each other has become solidified through the years, and they feel they have at last discovered a true home.

But Louis and Claudia's love is not to endure. Lestat, of course, is not really dead, and he has followed Louis and Claudia to Paris with his new lover, a young musician. Claudia turns from Louis to an older woman vampire, Madeleine, a sort of mother figure for the vampire child, and Louis becomes enchanted with Armand, a Parisian vampire.

The climax occurs with the burning of the theater. Only Louis and Armand are left as survivors, and Louis parts from Armand to return to America, reconciled to his lonely existence as a vampire with eternal life. As the vampire comes to the end of his story, the boy who has listened to all of it in fascination begs Louis to make him a vampire too.

On publication *Interview with the Vampire* became a best-seller and received varied reactions from the critics. One of the most glowing appeared in the *Wall Street Journal*: "It is hard to praise sufficiently the originality Miss Rice has brought to the age-old, ever-popular vampire tradition: it is undoubtedly the best thing in that vein since Bram Stoker, commanding peer status with 'Dracula.' She has gone off boldly on a tack altogether her own, with assurance, an incredibly controlled craftsmanship for a first novel, and a Gothic style of lustrous polish."[7]

Other critics were less enthusiastic, although most were balanced and fair in their comments. A few, such as Pearl Bell, simply didn't like the book: "Much as I admired Rice's powerful imagery, the impeccable authority of her prose, the novel seems a long-winded and floridly monotonous ordeal, all talk and no terror; I could grasp no clear sense of what her morally queasy, intolerably self-preoccupied vampire is meant to convey about the dark underside of mortal life. Perhaps this coven of gabby vampires is a grotesque emblem of the Faustian craving for immortality, for unlimited sexual potency, but who can be sure?"[8]

A number of reviewers had problems zeroing in on the meaning of Rice's book. Some critics do like to categorize fiction in order to apply the appropriate descriptors. Another critic, Edith Milton, decided, "The hell with literary pretensions and Gothic formulae. *Interview with the Vampire* is an erotic novel, where the sucking of blood has replaced more reproductive activities. So what's wrong with that? Dracula was always a bit of a seducer; if you go by recent movies, the vampire kiss is just an epidermal expression of a *Deep Throat* impulse."[9]

The Vampire Lestat

Rice's vampire series continued with *The Vampire Lestat,* published in 1985. Lestat is back and rather cross with Louis, the narrator of *Interview,* for not telling the truth about him. Therefore Lestat must occasionally backtrack to present a more truthful version of events, as well as recount his new adventures in present-day America as a rock star. He is also determined to locate Louis again and has decided the easiest way to do so is to become famous as quickly as possible and let Louis come to him.

The first part of the book, however, tells of Lestat's early life and how he became a vampire. A younger son in an impoverished aristocratic family in eighteenth-century France, Lestat becomes a vampire and finds he can save his beloved mother from death by making her a vampire too. The transformation causes her to grow fresh and appealing to Lestat, and they become vampire lovers in addition to being mother and son. Curious about the roots of vampirism, Lestat makes a time trip back to ancient Egypt and discovers the origins of his kind in an ancient earth-goddess cult.

Lestat in this book is certainly more likable than he was in *Interview,* and his adventures are interesting. In some ways this is the most successful of Rice's vampire books. The retelling of *Interview* by Lestat, his account of the story from that first book, is brief yet poignant. Hearing from Lestat why he did what he did, we realize that much of his supposed evil was inspired by love. And, as Lestat says,

> I betrayed [Louis] when I created him, that is the significant thing. Just as I betrayed Claudia. And I forgive the nonsense

he wrote, because he told the truth about the eerie contentment
he and Claudia and I shared. . . .

And I cannot say even now that I regret Claudia, that I wish
I had never seen her, nor held her, nor whispered secrets to her,
nor heard her laughter echoing through the shadowy gas-
lighted rooms of that all too human town house in which we
moved amid the lacquered furniture and the darkening oil
paintings and brass flowerpots as living beings should. Claudia
was my dark child, my love, evil of my evil. Claudia broke my
heart.[10]

Louis does turn up finally, and in the closing pages of the novel
Lestat believes his music has stirred the long-sleeping cult
mother from Egypt, Akasha. The finale is similar to that in *Interview:* a great fire destroys many vampires at a rock concert,
but Lestat and Louis escape.

Vampire lore and customs are important in Rice's vampire series. The creation of an elaborate subculture's traditions becomes
integral to the stories she is telling and helps explain the characters' complexities and the rules by which they must live. And
although Rice believes in many psychic phenomena, such as astral projection, out-of-the-body experiences, and ghosts, she does
not believe in vampires. As reported in a *Los Angeles Times* interview on 18 August 1988, she said, "But the one thing I find no
evidence for are vampires. That is pure mythology, pure dream."[11]

Queen of the Damned

Having lured the reader of the Vampire Chronicles into liking
Lestat in the previous book, Rice gives Lestat another chance to
get really bad. In *Queen of the Damned* Lestat discovers that he
has indeed awakened Akasha, the first vampire, who has been
inactive for 6,000 years. Akasha wants Lestat to join her in her
plan to eliminate most men on earth—vampires and others—so
that women can take over and bring about a world with lasting
peace. Banded against the evil queen are some good vampires,
including Louis, Gabrielle, and Armand. Finally Lestat joins the
good vampires, and the evil Akasha is defeated, but not without
considerable efforts described in a rather complicated plot involving a secret society and a collective dream about redheaded twins.

The love-hate interplay between Louis and Lestat continues in *Queen,* perfectly illustrated by the closing words of Lestat: "'Yes, I know,' I said, loving to look at him, to see the anger pumping him so full of life. 'And I love to hear you say it, Louis. I need to hear you say it. I don't think anyone will ever say it quite like you do. Come on, say it again. I'm a perfect devil. Tell me how bad I am. It makes me feel so good!'"[12]

An interesting touch with this novel is Rice's use of the poems of her husband, Stan Rice, throughout.

Kirkus found the book disappointing,[13] but Carl Hendricks in *Rave Reviews* said, "The author . . . has the perfect voice for the horror genre. Eerie, sensuous, violent, and erotic, *The Queen of the Damned* is a winner."[14] The *New York Times* reviewer did not seem to be fond of vampires but said, "Anne Rice is a writer of enormous ability. She has a masterly way with language, works on a broad canvas, has a vast range of knowledge, brings exotic settings vividly to life and is wonderfully clever, but these gifts are wasted on vampires. May she find subjects worthy of her talents before these dead guys suck her dry."[15]

Anne Rice likes her vampires, however, and is working on the fourth novel of the Vampire Chronicles, another story about Lestat, tentatively titled *The Body Thief.* The vampire books have been optioned for movies, but no films have been produced to date. Rice fancies Rutger Hauer as Lestat (Anne-Cassata, 32).

The Mummy

Part of the allure of monsters seems to be that not only do we find their awfulness fascinating in some perverse way but also we envy a trait held in common by many—immortality. The plot of many monster books and movies revolves around finding the only way to somehow put the monsters to rest and make them stop bothering us. Vampires are clearly the most sophisticated and sexually appealing, but other monster types have claims to immortality too.

A more recent arrival to the monster hall of fame is the

mummy, born with the relatively modern science of archaeology. Ancient Egyptian curses, mysteriously wrapped bodies destined for immortality, and hidden tombs full of treasures made this legend popular. The monster of the legend is the gauze-wrapped mummy, a creature that can be resurrected in order to avenge tomb robbers; punish impudent, unfeeling archaeologists; and satisfy sexual yearnings by snatching nubile young maidens.

It is not surprising that Anne Rice turned to a mummy for the subject of a book published in 1989. Part of her dedication in the book reads, "And lastly to my father Howard O'Brien who came more than once to get me from the neighborhood show, when 'the mummy' had scared me so badly that I couldn't even stay in the lobby with the creepy music coming through the doors."[16]

Rice had originally written *The Mummy* as a concept for a television miniseries but eventually became so disillusioned with the Hollywood process that she published the material as a book.[17] The miniseries, though, may still materialize.

Rice's mummy is no clunky zombielike creature from a Hollywood B movie. Rather, her mummy is an aristocrat—Ramses II himself. In the tradition of the curse of King Tut's tomb, an English Egyptologist, Lawrence Stratford, opens Ramses' tomb, ignoring the inscription, which states:

> Robber of the Dead, Look away from the tomb lest you wake its occupant, whose wrath cannot be contained. Ramses the Damned is my name. . . .
> Be Warned: I sleep as the earth sleeps beneath the night sky or the winter's snow; and once awakened, I am servant to no man. (*Mummy*, 3, 4)

Lawrence arranges to have the mummy shipped to his home in London and is murdered by his nephew, Henry.

Lawrence's lovely, virginal daughter, Julie, is now possessed of both great wealth and the mummy. She installs the mummy in her London home, where Ramses awakens and rips off his bandages. He is handsome, strong, and smart, and he stops nasty Henry from doing in Julie for her fortune. Ramses becomes quickly attuned to life in Edwardian London, and Julie finally gives in to her lustful feelings for him. Ramses, however, is still yearning for Cleopatra, for it seems he had found the secret of eternal life and had roamed the earth for centuries, taking to his tomb only after Cleo ditched him for Mark Antony.

Ramses uses his magical elixir to bring Cleo back to life. Her centuries of slumber, however, have not improved her basic drives. She thinks casual sex is fun, and murder gives her a thrill. Julie is faithful to Ramses, who finally offers her eternal life with him by drinking the elixir. She chugs it right down, of course. But you can't keep a bad one like Cleo down, and in the book's final pages she is discovered in an African backwater by a doctor who is immediately lured into her hospital bed.

More mummy books are under consideration, no doubt including the further adventures of Ramses, Julie, and Cleo. The vampire novels and *The Mummy* are being serialized as comic books/graphic novels.

In general, reviewers have not been as favorable to this book, but most of those critics concede that Rice's many fans will enjoy this title as well as the vampire books: "In fact, the only thing really dead here is much of Ms. Rice's prose. She favors a mock-epic style that went out with Rafael Sabatini. She evokes Conan Doyle and H. Rider Haggard, but when they wrote this way, they were serious. . . . If this sort of thing didn't appeal to you before, there isn't much reason to start. On the other hand, if you liked her vampires, you're going to love her mummies."[18] Another reviewer commented, "The characters are mostly boring and the conflict is flimsy. You know nothing bad is going to happen to anybody—and nothing does. You're also cheated out of a genuine conclusion, which is both dissatisfying and unfair. Stick to those blood drinkers, Anne, and let the sleeping mummies lie."[19]

Rice was originally hurt by negative reviews, particularly those in San Francisco when she first started publishing. She now seems able to be unconcerned about reviews and develops her new books based on her instincts, not critical advice: "From the beginning, the reviews were unbelievably vicious. *The New York Times* critic said the vampires talked like comic-book villains. But I kept doing the crazy things I felt I had to do, it worked out, and

I feel great. It's made me an optimist, and the cult following for the vampire books signifies that I chose the right course" (Holditch, 88).

Chelsea Quinn Yarbro: Can Monsters Be Humanized?

> I get a tremendous kick out of vampires. My vampires are just regular people who just happen to be vampires. . . . They are monsters but they don't have to act like them. They have that option.[20]
>
> —Chelsea Quinn Yarbro

Born and bred in California, Chelsea Quinn Yarbro had wanted to be a writer since childhood but turned to professional writing for pay only after her family's cartography business failed in 1970. She was quickly successful, writing not only horror fiction but fantasy, short stories, mysteries, westerns, and science fiction. Quinn Yarbro[21] is a prolific author, having written more than 40 novels, as well as novellas and numerous short stories, to date. She has used pseudonyms—Terry Nelsen Bonner and Vanessa Pryor. A believer in psychic phenomena, she has also written a series of factual books—the Michael series—about channeling through a Ouija board. Musically talented as well, Yarbro has written musical compositions, such as "Stabat Mater," "Alpha and Omega," and "Mythologies."[22]

Like Anne Rice, Yarbro is best loved for her vampire stories. Vampires are appealing beings. As Stephen King (himself the author of a vampire story, 'Salem's Lot) says regarding the popularity of vampires, "When all else is said and done, it's a chance to show women in scanty nightclothes, and guys giving the sleeping ladies some of the worst hickeys you ever saw, and to enact, over and over, a situation of which movie audiences never seem to tire: the primal rape scene."[23]

Yet again like Anne Rice, Yarbro does not embed her vampire stories in the usual Hollywood visions of bloodsuckers. Instead, she relies on the horrors of history to illustrate her basic premise that vampires are not necessarily bad in themselves. The delicate

Chronology: Chelsea Quinn Yarbro's Life and Works

1942 Born 15 September in Berkeley, California, the daughter of Clarence Elmer, a cartographer, and Lillian (Chatfield) Elmer, an artist.

1960–1963 Attends San Francisco State College (now University).

1963–1970 Works as a cartographer.

1969 Marries Donald Paul Simpson, an artist and inventor.

1972 First short stories published.

1976 First novel, *Time of the Fourth Horseman.*

1978 First of the Saint-Germain series, *Hotel Transylvania.*

1982 Divorces.

1987 First of the Olivia series, *A Flame in Byzantium.*

bloodsucking in which her vampires engage seems almost harm-less beside the bestial acts perpetrated by human beings. Yarbro says, "I call my books historical novels because to me, it's the his-tory that's horrifying, not the vampires" (Perdone, 49).

The Hotel Transylvania Series

Yarbro's five-volume set called the Hotel Transylvania series is based on a true historical figure. During the reign of Louis XV in France, appearing at the French court was a mysterious man, the Comte de Saint Germain, who claimed to be an accomplished alchemist and was thought by many to be immortal. His back-ground was shadowy, and the count dabbled in diplomatic in-trigue, which necessitated much travel and the fabrication of more stories.[24]

Although Yarbro's tales about the count range over many cen-turies, the first one published is set at the time the original count lived in Paris at the Hotel Transylvania. Yarbro has taken the few sketchy facts known about the real count and added more details, including his "true" identity as a vampire. Her writing device in this and the Olivia series is to include many letters and reports in the narrative, giving a tone of historical authenticity to these books.

In the first book, *Hotel Transylvania* (1978), the Comte de Saint Germain has arrived in Paris to restore an old family home, the Hotel Transylvania. He meets and becomes enamored of the beautiful, convent-bred Madelaine de Montalia. Madelaine is not merely a simple girl about to make her debut, however, for her father has promised her to satanists as a sacrifice. Though her father is no longer part of the evil coven, the satanists still want Madelaine. As a result, the plot rests on the count's efforts to save her, as well as on the romantic question of whether or not she loves the count enough to join him in a life of vampiric eternity. All turns out nicely in the end—but not before a thrilling climax of derring-do and threatened sadistic torture.

In the second book published about the count, *The Palace*

(1978), we go back in time to Renaissance Florence, where our hero is using the name Francesco Ragoczy de San Germano. Still an alchemist, Saint Germain hobnobs with the great figures of the era. This time his love object, Demetrice, turns to vampirism as an escape from being burned at the stake by Savonarola, a real life fanatic. Avoiding the evil schemes of this wicked man keeps our protagonist busy, and in the end Savonarola is himself burned at the stake as a heretic. Demetrice leaves Saint Germain, but throughout the book there have been letters to Saint Germain from Lady Olivia, obviously a past love.

Going back still farther in time for the third Saint Germain book, Yarbro spins a tale of imperial Rome in *Blood Games* (1979). Now a supplier of entertainers for Nero's court, Saint Germain falls in love with the beautiful Atta Olivia Clemens. Olivia's husband, Justus, gets sexual thrills from having Olivia raped and abused by rough gladiators as he watches. All the savage brutality of the Roman circus games are portrayed in graphic detail. Yet the love of Saint Germain and Olivia survives the carnage.

In *Path of the Eclipse* (1989), the next title in the series, Saint Germain is heading home to Transylvania from China. Busily trying to enhance his skills in the apothecary arts, Saint Germain finds further adventures in Tibet and India. Along the way he views the invasion of China by Genghis Khan's troops. The climax takes place during a sacrificial scene to the goddess Kali, wherein Saint Germain narrowly escapes ending up as dead meat on the altar.

In *Tempting Fate* (1982), the fifth Saint Germain book, Europe in the 1920s seems to be a good time and place for a busy vampire. After rescuing a widow and orphan in Russia, the count retires to his villa in Bavaria, where he watches the early formative stages of the German Nazi party. When the orphan girl he saved in Russia is bludgeoned to death by a thug, Saint Germain swears revenge. His former love from the first book, Madelaine de Montalia, provides assistance—not that she doesn't have problems of her own. In the end all comes about as much as it can for a vampire facing eternity.

The series at this point reaches its finale with *The Saint-Ger-*

main Chronicles (1983), consisting of five short stories. Here the adventures of Saint Germain are continued to the present, with settings in Europe and the American Southwest. The final story, "Renewal," is a reaffirmation of Saint Germain's compassion for humanity. Yarbro is reported to be continuing the series with a book entitled *Out of the House of Life.* In an essay on the Hotel Transylvania books Gil Fitzgerald concludes, "It is the combination of these themes—the dark side of the human soul and the loneliness of the immortal vampire who must witness the effects of that darkness, century after century—which gives the Saint Germain novels their strength. Yarbro reveals, through the rich tapestry of history, the depths to which man can sink, and the heroism and love. . . . Saint Germain, immortal and ever compassionate, is a testimony to the survival of hope."[25]

The Olivia Series

Rather than continuing to focus her vampire books on Saint Germain, Yarbro has made Atta Olivia Clemens the central character in her next vampire novels. Starting with *A Flame in Byzantium* (1988), Olivia's story picks up 500 years after her first appearance in *Blood Games.* Since her beloved Rome is under attack by one of many barbarian hordes, Olivia leaves for Byzantium, then the center of civilization. Accompanied by her faithful vampire servant, Niklos, she sets up housekeeping and anxiously awaits the time she can return to Rome. But single women of wealth are seemingly always suspect, throughout history, and Olivia is sentenced to death. She escapes, however, and at book's end leaves for Alexandria to try to rescue what texts may remain after the destruction of the once-great library there.

More centuries pass, and Olivia in *Crusader's Torch* (1988) is now residing in Tyre but eager to return to her beloved Rome. The third crusade is about to erupt in the Middle East, and Olivia wants to go home. Travel for a woman in the late twelfth century isn't easy, though, and so Olivia must engage the services of a handsome young knight, Valence Rainaut, who is in love with her.

Their journey is fraught with peril and made more exciting by the growing attraction between them. They consummate their passion, yet theirs cannot be a love eternal. Eventually Olivia does get back home, where she and Niklos, her servant, hope for a peaceful existence.

The last volume in the Olivia series, *A Candle for D'Artagnan* (1989), finds Olivia still living in Rome with Niklos. She is soon sent to France to help the pope gain his objective of having Mazarin appointed chief minister of the country on the death of the ailing Richelieu. In Paris she meets the Three Musketeers and their companion, D'Artagnan. Olivia and the young man eventually become lovers, but at book's end Olivia dies the true death for vampires, and Saint Germain writes in a letter to Niklos, "It may be twenty years since her death, but for me the place continues to be full of Olivia. She haunts the ruins, and I am not yet prepared to disturb her, though I know it is my memories I would disturb, and not Olivia, who is gone from me forever now. . . . The single consolation I can have for comfort is knowing that she found what I still seek—love that knows wholly and still loves. At least she had that before the true death came. If I am as fortunate, I will think my nearly four thousand years well spent."[26]

Yarbro's vampires, like those of Anne Rice, are likable beings. They seem reluctant to inflict vampirism on others. To cite Carol A. Senf, "According to Yarbro's interpretation, the vampire is no longer a cruel mirror of mankind's worst violence, but a cultured outsider who observes and comments on this cruelty."[27]

In comparing Chelsea Quinn Yarbro and Anne Rice, note that Yarbro's books dwell more on historical detail and that Rice's are more concerned with the inner thoughts and feelings of her vampires. One vampire literary expert, Brian J. Frost, describes Yarbro's vampire books as written in a "lush, romantic style," whereas Rice's novels are "generally depressing and morbid in tone."[28] Readers of both authors may wish to compare one style of describing vampires with the other, arguing the merits thereof, but both styles can be enjoyed for what they are. Both authors obviously subscribe to Senf's theory that in this century vampires can be shown to be basically attractive.[29] More to the point would be comparing the humanity of the vampires as depicted by both authors with the bestiality of human beings.

Yarbro's Other Monsters

Given her prolificness, Yarbro has created many memorable inhuman characters. Two such characters are classic figures in horror fiction: the werewolf and the zombie. Both are popular figures today in books and movies.

The Werewolf

According to Twitchell, "The werewolf is every bit as old as the vampire; in fact, he seems related, if not by blood, then by behavior. Not only are they both quiescent by day and molesters by night, and not only are they both excited by the moon and incited by women, they also transmit their obsession by biting. . . . However, the one attribute that separates the werewolf from other monsters is that a werewolf is created out of a man who *wants* to be possessed" (Twitchell, 208).

Movie star Vincent Price has written a book about monsters with his son, V. B. Price. They suggest the reason people are intrigued by werewolves is that werewolves are figures of human anxiety. The Prices maintain that "though it's not possible to say for sure if there's a common denominator to the anxiety [werewolves] spread, some of it must be related to the seemingly universal need humans have to distinguish themselves from nature and other beasts. Even people who have never heard of evolution like to see themselves as being a cut above the brutalities of nature. So when a human individual—that symbolic paragon of civility and superiority—suddenly takes on the characteristics of bestial monster, the fear it generates is intensified by shock, embarrassment, and indignation. And that's what makes good movies."[30]

The wolf villain is a familiar figure in fairy tales and folktales; the werewolf has starred in many horror stories and movies. Yarbro has written about one of the most pitiful werewolves in *The*

Godforsaken, a sad tale of a man who fights his fate of metamorphosis once a month when the moon is full. It is a dark and terrible tale of tragedy.

In sixteenth-century Spain Rolon, the crown prince, is a sweet-tempered, sensitive young man, secretly despised by his father, King Alonzo, for his gentleness. Alonzo would prefer that his bastard son, Gil, be his heir, and in order to get the church to legitimize Gil, Alonzo agrees to step up the Inquisition. The king and his family are already under a curse for their cruel activities, and it is poor Rolon who will pay. On a hunting expedition Rolon slowly realizes that he is the werewolf terrorizing the area and, knowing he must soon marry his intended—the daughter of the Doge of Venice—is in despair.

Alonzo, realizing he must get rid of Rolon altogether if Gil is to succeed him as king, arranges for Rolon to be framed for heresy and burned at the stake. Rolon escapes from prison as a werewolf and manages to kill Gil before he himself is slain.

In her Rolon/werewolf character Yarbro has presented another likable monster. She succeeds in answering her own questions about monsters: "I've also wondered over the years in my reading of horror stories—and I've enjoyed reading horror stories since I was about seven years old—what it is like for the object of horror to be what he or she or it is. Is there something intrinsic to the beastie itself, or is it a matter of reaction? And assuming such things did exist, how would they manage in the world? How would they escape detection and what would their lives be like?" (*Signs,* 186).

The critics liked this book for the most part, calling it "well drawn"[31] and "impressively ambitious."[32] One reviewer, Audrey Eaglen, said, "For them [young adults] it will be a gripping read, beautifully written, and suspenseful to the last of its nearly 400 pages."[33]

The Zombie

In the novelization of the movie *Dead & Buried* Yarbro has written about another kind of monster character—the living dead. Most zombies don't have a whole lot of sophistication or appeal about them. As Twitchell says, "The zombie myth seems flawed by its lack of complexity. The zombie is really a mummy in street clothes with no love life and a big appetite. Both are automatons; neither is cunning nor heroic. They simply lumber about (Karloff called it 'my little walk') shuffling their feet like dateless high school students before the prom. As opposed to the vampire, who is crafty, circumspect, and erotic, these two cousins are subhuman slugs" (Twitchell, 261).

Zombies are not ghosts, for with ghosts it is their spirits, or souls, that somehow appear to living mortals. With zombies, nothing spiritual is involved; it is the rotting bodies that appear.

If what Twitchell says about zombies is true, it must be a terrific challenge for an author like Yarbro to make them into sympathetic monsters. In addition, Yarbro must take a movie script written by someone else and turn it into a readable novel. Yarbro succeeds, for she is a skillful writer, and, too, the film *Dead & Buried* was not a run-of-the-mill, Karloff-shuffle zombie movie.

Dan Gillis is the sheriff of Potter's Bluff, a seemingly typical New England village. A series of bizarre murders are taking place in town, however, and some of the longtime inhabitants of the community, including Dan's wife, Janet, are acting strange. It turns out that the village mortician has been reactivating corpses into zombies; the town is full of the walking dead and among them is Janet. The final shocker is the last scene, in which Dan realizes that he himself is also a zombie. At the novelization's end Yarbro's matter-of-fact prose somehow make the scene even more shocking:

> Dan shook his head and took a step backward. His ankle and knee collapsed under him, and he looked stupidly down at them, at the end of the femur poking through rotten flesh and torn cloth. He reached out to cover it and the skin crumbled from his palm. His eyes were flat, he could no longer speak.
>
> "Come on, Dan," Dobbs said indulgently as he came toward him. "Let me fix that up for you."[34]

This concept presents a variation on the monsters previously described, for the horror of discovering that one has been functioning not as a human being but as a zombie would be soul-shattering. A good and scary story, we conclude, and more proof that Yarbro is a fine author. As she herself says, "Language is not an end in itself, but a means, a channel that a writer must, by the nature of the art, use. Beyond that, the words should not get in the way of the reader building the story in his or her head" (Wiloch, 502).

6. Satanism, Cults, and Teens

Teens like to investigate new ideas. They want to learn new and different things. They are at a point in their lives when they want to make decisions and become adults. They sometimes rebel against the ideals and beliefs of their parents and those in authority. They crave power, personal power, to do the things they want to do. They want to feel that they belong and that they are accepted by their peers. Teens are going through a complicated time of life.

In this search for identity as young adults teens sometimes turn to groups that promise the gift of power and the happiness of belonging to a special group. This is a time when teens join fraternities and sororities, as is the case with Lois Duncan's girls in *The Daughters of Eve*. Sometimes teens join informal social groups or become initiated into urban gangs. And sometimes they join more exotic groups, usually referred to by the general term *cults*.

Cults may be based on existing religious beliefs, such as those coming out of Asian religions. Some may appear to be based on Eastern mysticism but in reality have been established solely by sophisticated and unscrupulous con artists, such as the Bhagwan Osho Shree Rajneesh. Two groups of particular interest are based on older established religions—satanism and santería. Satanism is founded as an opposite belief system to Judeo-Christian belief; santería is a syncretic belief system that evolved from African religions and somewhat synthesized with Christian beliefs. Both have attracted much attention in the past decade from adults as well as teens—those who are involved in the cults, those who are victims of the cults and their actions, and also law enforcement officers and therapists. Although because these groups are secretive it is difficult to ascertain what activity is actually taking place and how much real involvement there is, it is obvious that satanism and santería are being practiced today.

Public reaction to the growth of satanism and santería seems to be divided into three groups: (a) those—such as parents and teachers—who believe that such growth is exaggerated and that most people involved are simple experimenters; (b) those who must take it seriously, such as police officers and therapists; and (c) those who seem panicked over the idea, such as media sensationalists and religious fundamentalists.

An example of the last-named group is well illustrated by Geraldo Rivera's now-infamous television program on teens and satanism, which seemed to be based on this logic:

1. If kids listen to heavy-metal music, they will become druggies.
2. If kids become druggies, they will turn to satanism.
3. If kids become satanists, they will become murderers.[1]

It is true that teens and adults with existing personality disorders can become obsessed with ideas like satanism. In these cases satanism is a symptom, not the cause. One of the teen murderers featured on the Geraldo Rivera television show, Sean Sellers, admits to strange obsessions: "'I was just wrapped up in my own darkness,' he says. 'I would just lose all compassion. I didn't care about anything. I fantasized about chopping people up in little pieces.'"[2] Sean blames satanism for his crime of killing his parents. He says he is now a born-again Christian and repents of his actions; he believes that Satan exists as an entity and that Satan possessed him. Sean is now on death row in Oklahoma.

Of all the calls received by the Cult Awareness Network in Chicago, more deal with satanism than with any other cult. Newspapers and television report on apparently satanic crimes. Occult symbolism can be found as graffiti marked on city walls. Mutilated animals and inverted crosses are discovered in deserted rural areas. There is a growing acceptance of the reality of satanic practices.

At a conference for law enforcement agents and counselors dealing with satanism and the law, four levels of involvement were defined by Jerry Simandl of the Chicago Police Department:

1. Experimental stage—dabblers
2. Nontraditional—self-styled
3. Organized traditional
4. Occultic networking[3]

The stage of least involvement, experimental, is the point at which some teens may first get interested and involved. Wearing the accoutrements of rock stars, engaging in sataniclike rites, and even getting involved in animal sacrifice are not unusual at this stage. It is a time of experimentation and "fooling around."

The second stage, nontraditional and self-styled satanism, is often more dangerous, since someone with an already-serious personality disorder may devise a personal belief system to try to gain power and tie it in some vague way to satanism. Such persons—adults and teens—are often seeking control and come up with their own ideas of how to get power, sometimes based on the readily available works by Anton LaVey, founder of the Church of Satan in San Francisco.[4]

The third stage, traditional organized satanism, means joining a group, perhaps a coven, of people seeking power through a belief system. These people may be followers of Anton LaVey, or they may adopt other styles of satanism, such as those inspired by Aleister Crowley, an English occultist, some years ago. At this point the satanic group becomes a cult by definition and encompasses many characteristics of destructive cults, such as the presence of a charismatic leader and group binding through crime. Human sacrifice may be demanded by such a group.

The last stage of satanic involvement, occultic networking, has little factual corroboration. It is thought that one or more satanic occult networks may be at work. One such, "The Process," may be a satanic cult responsible for the Tate murders and other crimes, such as the "Son of Sam" killings. Such networks may be involved with drug distribution and other criminal activities, as well as with bizarre crimes associated with satanic practice.[5]

Another term sometimes used in connection with cults is *witchcraft*. Witchcraft, however, is more complex, in that, like santería, it should not always be associated with evil. Satanism is always viewed as an evil belief system. Whether based on Judeo-Christian tenets or on individual power grabbing, satanism is practiced for the good of no one except the members of the cult, who believe that evil, rather than good, will triumph.

Many books, nonfiction and fiction, have been written about satanism. One of the best-known writers to use this theme is Dennis Wheatley, a British author who wrote stories about basically good and decent people fighting the demonic powers of darkness. In novels like *The Devil Rides Out,* in which the Duc de Richleau battles the evil Mocato for the souls of his friends, Wheatley presents a picture of satanism that is real and threatening. He has influenced many authors, and his name is still used to describe those kinds of books which present the devil and the demons of hell as very real, and satanists as very nasty people.

Rosemary's Baby

One book has been responsible in large part for sparking the surge in popularity of occult literature in the past 25 years: Ira Levin's *Rosemary's Baby,* published in 1967. It quickly became a best-seller, and the movie that followed, directed by Roman Polanski (husband of Sharon Tate), was a box-office smash.

Rosemary's Baby is a story of satanism as seen through the eyes of a rather naive young woman, Rosemary. She is married to Guy Woodhouse, an actor, for whom she left the Catholic Church of her upbringing. As the novel opens, the Woodhouses have the opportunity to move into a wonderful historic apartment building in New York City called the Bramford.

An old neighbor of Rosemary's, Hutch, warns the young couple against their new home. The Bramford, he tells them, has seen much unsavory history, including cannibalism from the infamous Trench sisters and the lynching of an acknowledged satanist, Adrian Marcato, not to mention entirely too many suicides. But Guy and Rosemary think Hutch is being needlessly nervous and move into the Bramford anyway.

Both Guy and Rosemary want more in their lives. Guy wants the break that will allow him to succeed in his career, rather than existing on the fringes of the theater world and earning his only real money by doing commercials. Rosemary wants a baby.

Once settled in their new apartment, Rosemary meets a young woman, Terry, in the laundry room. Terry, a reformed drug addict, is staying with an elderly couple in the Bramford, the Castevets, who have helped her turn her life around. Terry shows Rosemary the pretty pendant the Castevets have given her, an antique silver charm filled with an herb, tannis root.

Shortly thereafter Rosemary and Guy are shocked when Terry jumps out of a window at the Bramford, killing herself. They meet her mentors, Roman and Minnie Castevet, who turn to the Woodhouses for comfort and companionship. At first the Woodhouses find the Castevets not only funny and peculiar but nosy and pushy. But Guy, somewhat to Rosemary's surprise, claims to like them, and the old and young couples settle into being friendly neighbors.

Rosemary's life, however, is not perfect. She still wants a baby, and she has strange dreams, some of which hinge on her guilt for marrying a non-Catholic. She also hears funny noises through the wall from the Castevets' apartment. Minnie Castevet gives Rosemary the charm that had once been Terry's, but Rosemary tucks it away in a drawer because of the pungent odor. Rosemary isn't pregnant yet, and Guy spends too much time with the Castevets; still, Rosemary doesn't want to irritate him by complaining, since he has just lost an acting role he wanted badly.

Then things start to happen. The actor to whom Guy has lost the part is struck blind, and Guy gets the part after all. In delight, Guy suggests to Rosemary that they work on having a baby. On the night conception looks probable, Rosemary prepares a special dinner for them, and Minnie provides dessert, chocolate mousse. Rosemary falls asleep heavily and has a bizarre dream in which a demonlike Guy rapes her. In the morning she discovers to her discomfort that Guy has proceeded with their plans despite her unconscious state.

Subsequently Rosemary is delighted to learn she is pregnant, and the happy Castevets arrange for her to go to Dr. Abraham Saperstein, a noted obstetrician and old friend. Dr. Abe asks Minnie to make a special herb concoction, including tannis, for Rosemary to drink. Rosemary starts to prepare for the baby's arrival but is bothered by a sharp and constant pain, which Dr. Abe assures her is quite normal.

Rosemary takes to wearing the good-luck charm Minnie gave her earlier and forces herself to drink the daily herb potion. She finds she craves raw meat, and one day she is appalled to catch a reflection of herself eating a raw chicken liver. Her pregnancy is well advanced when her friends tell her that her pain is not normal and that she should go to another doctor. This plan is upset, however, when Rosemary's old friend Hutch makes a date to see her but is felled by a stroke.

Guy's career is doing well; Rosemary feels the baby moving inside her, thus reassuring her that it is not dead. Eventually the pain goes away, and the baby's nursery is ready for the birth. Then Hutch dies.

Hutch's friend Grace Cardiff gives Rosemary a book, *All of Them Witches*. Hutch had murmured in a brief rousing from his coma for Grace to tell Rosemary that the name is an anagram. Rosemary is puzzled but takes tiles from her Scrabble set to see what she can deduce. The title of the book yields nothing, but then she notices a dog-eared page in the chapter on Adrian Marcato. The name of Marcato's son, Steven, is underlined. Sure enough, when Rosemary uses the tiles for Steven Marcato, she immediately gets Roman Castevet.

Rosemary is fascinated with other facts in the book and begins to theorize that the old couple next door and their friends are a coven of satanists who want her unborn baby to use in a human sacrifice. Guy is exasperated with this notion and throws the book away. Rosemary stops drinking Minnie's herbal concoction and voices some of her fears to Dr. Abe, who humors her. He tells her that Roman doesn't have long to live and that the Castevets plan shortly to visit some of their favorite cities before he dies. Dr. Abe gives Rosemary conventional vitamin pills, and the Castevets leave for Europe.

Somewhat happier, Rosemary is still suspicious. She accuses Guy of being part of the coven and takes her hospital suitcase to Dr. Abe's office. It is now nearly 25 June, and the birth is imminent. Rosemary has earlier disposed of her tannis-root charm; now the nurse in Dr. Abe's office remarks on its absence and then says she wishes the doctor would get rid of his aftershave lotion, which has the same smell.

Rosemary, realizing her doctor must be involved in the satanic conspiracy to get her baby, hauls her suitcase out into the sweltering weather. She convinces another doctor to see her, but this man, believing her to be suffering from delusions, calls Guy and Dr. Abe, who drag Rosemary home in disgrace.

Inside the Bramford Rosemary tries again to escape, but she goes into labor and gives birth to her baby at home. When she regains consciousness, she is told her baby was born dead. Yet she is not given medicine to dry up her milk, and she must manually extract it. She assumes it is thrown away. But several weeks later she hears a baby crying in the Bramford, and she hears ritualistic music in the Castevets' apartment next door.

Believing her baby to be still alive but in great danger of being sacrificed, Rosemary heads for the Castevets' apartment, a lethal kitchen knife clutched in her hand. She enters the Castevets' living room, where strange, Goyaesque paintings are hanging. In a bassinet draped in black she finds her baby. But he has strange yellow eyes with vertical irises, and, as she later finds out, he has budding horns, clawed hands, and hoofed feet. Her baby was never meant to be a sacrifice, for he is Satan's own child.

In the final pages of the book Rosemary considers killing herself and her baby by leaping from the window. Gradually, however, she is persuaded to be the satanic infant's real mother, and the reader's last view of Rosemary is her gentle presence leaning over the bassinet and coaxing her baby to smile.

This final scene is awful in its quiet evil, for the reader now knows that the little Satan stands a good chance of growing to maturity. He will undoubtedly treat his mother, Rosemary, as badly as, if not worse than, her husband, who allowed her to be used by the coven as a host for Satan's child. Rosemary is unlikely ever to find comfort in the religion of her youth, and probably she will be overwhelmed by guilt. Poor Rosemary.

This deceptively simple, fast-moving book deserved to be a best-seller. The critics seemed to be in agreement over Levin's skill as a writer, and although a few deplored the basic plot, it is easy to see why the public thought it was great. The reviewer for *Time* magazine summed it up well by saying, "Ultimately, there are two tests for any thriller or piece of horror fiction: 1) does the author play fair, yet come up with a shocker of a denouement? and 2) is the reader's willing suspension of disbelief rewarded with a final close-the-book aspiration of relief as he returns to his own world? Author Levin bats fifty-fifty. On the one hand, the ending of *Rosemary's Baby,* though inevitable, is flat; on the other hand, it is as unsettling as the first stirrings of a poison-ivy rash at the conclusion of a picnic."[6]

Indeed, one critic credits Levin with changing the "shape of the contemporary horror-fantasy tale, once and for all."[7] *Rosemary's Baby* remained on the best-seller lists longer than any other horror hardcover book from 1960 to 1988.[8]

The Exorcist

Another book followed *Rosemary's Baby* to the best-seller lists in 1971—*The Exorcist,* which proved again that the public likes to read books about horror. *The Exorcist* deals with another aspect of satanism, possession by demons. This theme fascinated people who read the book and those who later went to see the movie, in which Linda Blair starred as the possessed child.

The Exorcist, written by William Peter Blatty, is more horrible than *Rosemary's Baby* in its graphic descriptions yet provides a more positive ending. In *The Exorcist* good, as embodied by two Catholic priests, confronts the powers of hell and wins—at least for the time being. The victory is not an easy one, however.

The plot is straightforward. A star actress on location for a movie in Washington, D.C., has rented a Georgetown house for herself and her 11-year-old daughter, Regan. The actress, Chris MacNeil, slowly comes to realize that Regan is no longer her sweet child but is possessed by something evil and frightening. Medical science and psychiatry seem unable to deal with Regan's problem. A policeman, Lieutenant Kinderman, who is investigating a death in the neighborhood, becomes involved. In her desperation to make Regan well again Chris turns to a Jesuit psychiatrist, Father Karras, and finally voices her fear that Regan is possessed by a demon. Ultimately Father Merrin, an exorcism expert, is called in, and the two priests confront the evil power that has taken possession of Regan. They win only by Father Karras's self-sacrifice. He invites the demon to take him over, but in the brief instant before the possession is complete Karras throws himself from the window to his death.

Interesting questions are raised in *The Exorcist* about demonic possession in relation to modern psychiatric practices and theories, as well as attitudes of contemporary religious leaders about such ancient ideas. No firm answers are provided in the book, but the public's interest was aroused by the concept of demonic possession, and many books and movies picked up on this theme after the *The Exorcist's* success.

The Exorcist illustrates a common thought in historical and psychological literature about poltergeists, witchcraft, and possession. It has sometimes been theorized that young adolescents, especially girls, seem to have strange powers, on occasion resorting to hysteria and being able to cause strange, seemingly inexplicable events. This theory has somewhat fallen into disrepute, but it occasionally does crop up—for example, as an explanation for the Salem witchcraft accusations, trials, and executions in seventeenth-century New England.

Witchcraft

Satanism, in practice and in literature, is considered evil; there are no gray areas with satanism. Witchcraft, though, can be practiced for good or bad, and modern definitions of witchcraft seem to be placing the term on the side of good, along with pagan and wiccan practices. Witchcraft involves the use of magical belief systems supposedly to obtain power; how that power is used determines whether the witchcraft is good or bad. Historically in Europe and America witchcraft was considered evil, and the term *witchcraft* was synonymous with *satanism*. Since all non-Christian religions were considered heresy in more religiously oppressive societies, the term came to be synonymous with satanism. In modern usage, however, satanism and witchcraft are seen as different belief systems. Today witchcraft is more often viewed as a pagan, pre-Christian belief, rather than an anti-Christian belief like satanism. In the United States pagan-based witchcraft groups have been popular since the 1960s, a probable outgrowth of investigation of alternative religions during that period.

Apparently, however, through the ages the belief persisted, especially in Europe, that although witches were prosecuted for their ideas and practices, many were harmless berb gatherers and practitioners of simple medicinal cures. A favorite historical novel, *The White Witch,* by Elizabeth Goudge, was popular in America and Britain for many years; it told the story of a gypsy girl in Elizabethan England who was called a white witch. Some believed the white witches to have great power, an idea explored in books like Katherine Kurtz's *Lammas Night,* which tells how white witches protected Britain from invasion by the Nazis in World War II.

Nevertheless, paganism is not always benign, as is shown in *The Wicker Man,* a novelization by Robin Hardy and Anthony Shaffer, based on the film which seems in recent years to be gaining a cult[9] popularity. *The Wicker Man* tells of a rather prudish policeman who is investigating the disappearance of a missing girl on the island of Summerisle, off the coast of Scotland. Summerisle is the exclusive home of a pagan commune, and the policeman becomes increasingly fearful that the missing child is to be used as a sacrifice to guarantee a good harvest. The novel climaxes at a festival at which a hollow wicker man is to be burned with a virgin inside. In the end, it is the policeman who is the sacrifice, for the gender of the virgin doesn't matter.

Stephen King's short story "Children of the Corn" also uses the theme of corruption in pagan-type cults. In this story the teens of the title ritualistically kill anyone over the age of 19 as part of a grotesque earth/corn worship.

Another book of note that has enjoyed long popularity is Fritz Leiber's *Conjure Wife*. First published in 1953 by Twayne and made into three different film versions (all with different titles), *Conjure Wife* tells the story of Tansy, who uses voodoo to protect her husband and help him get ahead in his career as a college professor. In the highly political atmosphere of academe this does not seem to be a bad idea, but Tansy's husband forces her to stop. As it turns out, Tansy is not the only practitioner of magical arts on campus, and some thoroughly nasty types steal her soul as punishment for dabbling in witchcraft. In the end Tansy's husband must help her by using magical arts himself. This book illustrates the dichotomy of witchcraft as mentioned earlier, for in itself witchcraft is neither good nor bad; how it is used is what determines its definition. Tansy is a white witch, for she uses her power for good, but her enemies are black witches, for they use their power for evil. A more disturbing element in this book, at least for feminists, is the theme that in one way or another, all women practice witchcraft.[10]

Santería

Santería, too, can be used for good or evil. It is based on African religions, particularly beliefs of the Yoruba in Nigeria. When Africans were shipped to the New World as slaves, they were forbidden from practicing their traditional religions and were expected to adopt Christianity. The slaves seemingly acquiesced, but instead of adopting the new religion wholeheartedly they merely used it as a cover-up for continuing their own beliefs. The identities of the old African gods were applied to the Christian saints; when the slaves prayed to the saints, the masters did not know the slaves were actually praying to their old gods. The syncretic nature of this religion took on variations in different locations, variations that have different names. The best known, of course, is the voodoo of Haiti, but there are also obeah, condomblé, macumba, and others. One of the most mysterious beliefs has become known only recently in the United States, that of Palo Mayombe, brought here during the Cuban Boatlift of 1980. Based on African Congo, rather than Nigerian, beliefs, Palo Mayombe is a dark, scary religion teaching that human sacrifice can give its followers great protection.

Palo Mayombe received a great deal of publicity in 1989 with the discovery of a ritual murder in Matamoros, Mexico, across the border from Brownsville, Texas. Police on a drug raid discovered a grisly scene involving mutilation, murder, and evidence of brutal rituals. The leader of the perpetrators was a handsome, charismatic, bisexual man who had studied Palo Mayombe in order to gain its power to protect his drug business. This leader, Constanzo, in a suicide pact similar to that of Adolf Hitler, died with his lover after ordering followers to shoot them both before being taken by the police.[11]

One of the details that came to light in this case was that a commercial feature film, *The Believers,* had been used as an indoctrinational/educational film for new members of the cult. *The Believers,* released in 1987, starred Martin Sheen and was based on the book *The Religion,* by Nicholas Condé, published five years earlier.

The story of *The Religion/Believers* is a story of horror. A newly widowed anthropologist, Cal Jamison, moves to New York with his son, Chris. Cal's mentor, Kathryn Clay (a sort of Margaret Mead type), has found Cal a job teaching at Columbia University, and he gets an apartment and a housekeeper, Mrs. Ruiz, as well. It would seem that Cal and Chris are all set to enjoy a new life.

But Cal keeps seeing odd evidence in the city of the practice of santería, evidence that disturbs him for some unknown reason. Chris is not adjusting well to his new life or to his mother's death. Mrs. Ruiz behaves rather weirdly too.

Cal decides to make a serious, anthropological study of the practice of santería in the city. He quickly discovers it is more than a simple, harmless folk belief. Even the attractions of his new girlfriend, Torey, do not distract him from the disturbing aspects of santería. Mrs. Ruiz persists on placing santería-style protection charms around the apartment; Cal insists on their removal, and Mrs. Ruiz dies—it seems that santería is a powerful religion. Torey eventually admits she believes in it herself. Cal thinks he is doing a good deed by helping the police solve ritualistic child murders, but things are mounting to a point where he can no longer control events.

Even Cal's mentor, Kathryn Clay, seems to have entirely too much respect and fear for santería. Finally all the strange elements of the story come together, with Cal realizing that his son Chris has been chosen for a sacrifice to avert nuclear holocaust and that in order for the ritual to work Cal himself must kill his son. After astral battles on another plane of consciousness, Cal is able to save Chris, Torey, and himself from santería and they flee from the wicked city. The epilogue, however, makes it plain that there can be no escape.

The book was popular, being chosen as an alternate selection of the Literary Guild and the Doubleday Book Club. A few reviewers liked it, but *Kirkus* said rudely, "Familiar hooey, dished out with a few solid ghastlies, some tabloid research, and an unusual degree of talk pseudo-seriousness: only for readers who found *Rosemary's Baby* much too subtle or irreverent about devil-doings."[12]

Fantasy-Game Obsession

Law enforcement officers include with the destructive cults discussed earlier still another group, one inspired by so-called fantasy games, which involve role-playing identified with various mythologically inspired characters. A number of teen suicides have been linked to obsessive behavior with various fantasy games.[13] As with what occurs in other cults, such extreme behavior, including suicide, cannot be blamed on a game. Such games have possibly provided a mechanism for already-disturbed teens to manifest irregular behavior. Games, especially obsessive preoccupation with them, may be a symptom but are not the cause of emotional disturbance.

Sometimes appearing on recommended reading lists for high school students is William Dear's *The Dungeon Master: The Disappearance of James Dallas Egbert III,* which tells the true story of a young prodigy, away from home and in college at the age of 16. When the boy disappears from Michigan State University his parents hire, Dear, a private detective, (who in fact was Dear, the book's author) to try to find him. What the detective ultimately discovers is a mad maze created in the basements of MSU and, finally, Dallas himself. But the youth, caught up in the fantasy of his game life, is in precarious mental health and eventually ends his life by shooting himself.[14]

A fictional tale of a similar case was recounted by Rona Jaffe in *Mazes and Monsters,* a book later turned into a movie with Tom Hanks and Christopher Makepeace. Here four friends in college begin to take their leisuretime game, Mazes and Monsters, too seriously and start to act out their fantasy roles. One of the young men, Ronnie, is lost in some abandoned caverns near the school and suffers delusions that the game is real. In the end he is found, but his mind is seriously disturbed.

John Coyne has written a fictional fantasy on the same idea, called *Hobgoblin.* Hobgoblin is a fantasy game based on Irish mythology but played like other role-playing fantasy games. The protagonist, Scott Gardiner, has just lost his father and is having trouble adjusting to a new life and a new school. He grows insular and becomes heavily involved with his fantasy-game favorite. For Scott, his game too begins to become an obsession, but in his case the fantasy becomes real. In the end Scott returns to the world of the living, leaving his Hobgoblin game behind. This ending is happier than the true story of Dallas, but then *Hobgoblin* is a book of fantasy horror, not real life.

Alternate Belief Systems Today

The historical background of alternative belief systems is intriguing and illustrates the rich and varied cultural patterns of the world. In the United States today, however, alternative belief systems are generally suspected by mainstream society, and some, such as satanism, have rightly earned a reputation as evil. Although interest in such beliefs is not dangerous in itself, becoming obsessed with any subject—such as satanism—is often symptomatic of personality disorders. As with many things, it is a matter of degree: a healthy interest is fine, but total immersion may lead to disaster.

7. True Crime and Imagination: Three Books by Robert Bloch

In recent years horror literature, particularly that which is in the tradition of earlier writers like H. P. Lovecraft, has sometimes been called dark fantasy. Lovecraft (HPL), who penned ominous and mysterious works a half-century ago in New England, has inspired a devoted following among a body of writers who admire his ability to create mood and horror. Critics and reviewers even refer to certain works as being Lovecraftian, said particularly of works based on the idea of ancient evils. As Robert Bloch, a protégé of his, states in an introduction to Lovecraft's works, "In a time of turmoil there is a widespread intimation—not based on hereditary impulse but on today's realities—that the evils abroad in the world may come from without as well as from within ourselves. While we may consciously reject his cosmology [referring to HPL's Cthulhu Mythos] as absurd, a part of us finds in it a chilling confirmation of secret fears.[1]

During the middle years of the twentieth century Lovecraft inspired other writers, and when a teenager named Robert Bloch wrote to him after reading his stories in the now-famous magazine *Weird Tales,* Lovecraft encouraged the youngster to become a horror writer himself.

Though Lovecraft was greatly admired, with his death in 1937 his reputation seemed to be waning. August Derleth, himself a

121

writer of note, founded a publishing company, Arkham House, in Derleth's hometown of Sauk City, Wisconsin, for the purpose of preserving and proselytizing the works of H. P. Lovecraft and his followers.

Dark fantasy and horror literature continue today, with many writers, including Robert Bloch, having started their career by writing in the tradition of an earlier master.

Robert Bloch: Reality or Imagination, Which Is Worse?

> I think most of us like to be scared *safely*. There is that wonderful realization that once you close the book or turn off the television or leave the theater, you're back in a world in which you've escaped from all of the dangers that the characters in the story have faced. I believe this feeling of relief is intensified today by the realization that we don't always escape in the actual world about us.[2]
>
> —Robert Bloch

Robert Bloch can be considered typical of horror writers today in that he has combined a career of writing short stories and novels with creating scripts for the movies. In fact Bloch reports that his first real experience with fear was at a movie he attended alone at the age of nine, *The Phantom of the Opera,* starring Lon Chaney. He is also typical of those many writers in this century who have not limited themselves to any one genre, for he has written mainstream fiction, science fiction, fantasy, suspense, and mysteries, all in addition to horror literature.

Robert Bloch was born in Chicago in 1917 into a pleasant middle-class family. While he was still a youngster, the family moved to Milwaukee, Wisconsin. As a high school student Bloch was involved in a number of extracurricular activities, including drama. He was an avid reader and discovered the delights of horror in the movies and in the magazine *Weird Tales.* Particularly impressed by the stories of H. P. Lovecraft, the young Bloch wrote to the author, and a correspondence developed. Lovecraft encouraged the teenager to write; that encouragement led to Bloch's submission of stories to *Weird Tales.* His first published work was

Chronology: Robert Bloch's Life and Works

1917 Born 5 April in Chicago, the son of Raphael Bloch (a bank cashier) and Stella Loeb Bloch (a teacher).
1927 Family moves to Milwaukee, Wisconsin.
1933 Writes to H. P. Lovecraft.
1934 First story published.
1940 Marries Marion Holcombe. Daughter, Sally Ann, born.
1945 First collection of short stories, *The Opener of the Way,* published by Arkham.
1947 *The Scarf* (novel).
1953 Commences career as free-lance writer.
1954 *Spiderweb, The Kidnaper,* and *The Will to Kill* (novels).
1958 *Shooting Star* (novel), and short story collection, *Terror in the Night.*
1959 *Psycho.*
1960 Moves to Hollywood to become movie scriptwriter. Film version of *Psycho* released. Short story collection *Pleasant Dreams—Nightmares* published.
1961 *Firebug* (novel), and short story collection, *Blood Runs Cold.*
1962 *Terror* (novel).
1963 Divorces. Short story collection, *Bogey Men.*
1964 Marries Eleanor Alexander.
1970 Short story collection, *The Living Demons.*
1971 Short story collection, *Fear Today, Gone Tomorrow.*
1972 *Night-World* (novel).
1974 *American Gothic* (novel).
1977 Short story collections *The King of Terrors* and *Cold Chills.*
1978 Short story collection, *Out of the Mouths of Graves.*
1979 Short story collection, *Such Stuff as Screams Are Made Of.*
1982 *Psycho II.*
1984 *Night of the Ripper* (novel).
1987 Short story collection, *Midnight Pleasures.*
1988 *The Selected Stories of Robert Bloch.*
1989 *Lori* (novel), and short story collection, *Fear and Trembling.*
1990 *Psycho House* (novel).

"Lilies," in *Marvel Tales,* (1934).[3] Bloch's writing career was launched, and before long he was publishing stories in *Weird Tales,* as his mentor, Lovecraft, had done.

Then as now, struggling writers were unable to earn a good living until they were established as authors. After finishing high school during the Great Depression Bloch wanted a job but couldn't find one. In desperation he wrote stories, and some of them sold.[4] Later, in 1942, he became a copywriter for an ad agency in Milwaukee, a job that would last until 1953, when he felt able to concentrate on writing. Those years working at a conventional job were the years Bloch spent honing his skills as a writer. During that time some of his best-known short stories were published, including "Yours Truly, Jack the Ripper" (1943) and "Lizzie Borden Took an Axe" (1946). Both of these stories were inspired by real-life crimes, a theme Bloch would use throughout his writing career.

Psycho

About the time Bloch became a full-time writer, his family moved from Milwaukee to Weyauwega, Wisconsin, a small town not far from Plainfield. Most people, even natives of the state, had never heard of either town, but within a few years the world would know about Plainfield, the site of Ed Gein's horrible activities—crimes that would spark Bloch's interest and result in the creation of his best-known work, *Psycho.*

Ed Gein's real story is far worse than the tale Bob Bloch concocted. Even a splatterpunk writer, Richard Christian Matheson, years later described Ed Gein as, "sick, sick, sick."[5] The recent popularity of true-crime books has resulted in old, particularly bizarre crimes being resurrected, and the story of Ed Gein has been published in book form.[6] Norman Bates was nothing compared to Ed Gein, a murderer who dressed victims like deer, robbed graves, and allegedly committed necrophilia and cannibalism. That may be because Norman is in part, according to Stephen King, based on a folklore character, the werewolf, rather than a crazy murderer of today.[7]

Psycho was inspired by Ed Gein but was not based on his crimes per se. Bloch says: "I was just intrigued by the idea that a middle-aged man could live in such a small community for so many years and commit so many murders without the residents ever suspecting. I said to myself, 'There's a story there,' and made up a story. The details of the murders were not printed in the newspapers at the time. I didn't know them until many years later."[8]

Bloch's previously published novel *The Scarf* had early shown his ability to delve into the psychological makeup of twisted minds and souls. Certainly the character of Norman Bates is a masterpiece of schizophrenic madness, so much so that the character has become a piece of modern folklore, an icon epitomizing the Oedipus complex in contemporary society.

Psycho the Book

Alfred Hitchcock was remarkably faithful to Bloch's original book about a very strange man who loves his mother. Other than changing the locale and adding necessary dialogue, the movie plot remains quite true to the book's.

The story begins when Mary Crane swipes money from her boss and runs away with it. Lost on the road, she stops at the Bates Motel—a big mistake, as everyone knows. Norman Bates checks her in, making a number of comments about his mother that illustrate his fixation. Left alone in her motel room, Mary realizes how stupid she has been to steal the money and resolves to return it in the morning. She decides to take a shower, symbolic, in a way, of cleansing herself of her sin. The shower scene is one of the most famous in filmdom, discussed and analyzed at length by film historians and imitated by other film directors. As Bloch describes it in the book:

> That's why she didn't hear the door open, or note the sound of footsteps. And at first, when the shower curtains parted, the steam obscured the face.
> Then she *did* see it there—just a face, peering through the

curtains, hanging in midair like a mask. A head-scarf con-
cealed the hair and the glassy eyes stared inhumanly, but it
wasn't a mask, it couldn't be. The skin had been powdered
dead-white and two hectic spots of rouge centered on the cheek-
bones. It wasn't a mask. It was the face of a crazy old woman.

Mary started to scream, and then the curtains parted further
and a hand appeared, holding a butcher knife. It was the knife
that, a moment later, cut off her scream.

And her head.[9]

Norman is shocked when he finds the body but knows he has
to cover up what he is sure is his mother's crime. Mary's sister,
Lila, is horrified when she hears of her sister's murder. She too
goes to the Bates Motel, determined to find out who is responsible
for Mary's death, as does Mary's boyfriend, Sam. The two try to
get at the truth of Mary's murder, ending in a search of the Bates's
home, a creepy old mansion next to the motel. Lila is sure Norman's mother is the key to the crime and wants to talk to her. Lila
thinks she finds old Mrs. Bates in the fruit cellar. She sees a grotesque figure there, one who cries:

"I am Norma Bates," said the high, shrill voice. And then there
was the hand coming out, the hand that held the knife . . . and
the knife came up, quick as death. . . .

Lila closed her mouth, but the scream continued. It was the
insane scream of a hysterical woman, and it came from the
throat of Norman Bates. (*Psycho*, 208)

Now we know: schizophrenic Norman has been playing the part
of his mother because his disturbed mind cannot deal with the
idea of her death. She has been an ever-dominant force in his life,
and Norman cannot exist without her. One critic has the following explanation for the strength of *Psycho* as a story: "The power
lies in Bloch's ability to manipulate our uncertainties: although
quite early on we learn that Bates's version of his mother's life/
death does not square with other known facts, the reasons for this
discrepancy remain in doubt until the *denouement*."[10]

It is unfortunate that the fame of the film makes it impossible
to read the book as a fresh experience. Bloch wrote from Norman's
perspective, and although clues about the real identity of Mrs.

Bates are present, those who are unaware of the story of Norman or of Ed Gein would surely be surprised and shocked, perhaps even horrified, by this final plot twist. As Randall D. Larson says, "It isn't easy to evaluate *Psycho* as a book in the shadow of the film, but taken by itself, it remains a remarkable and well-told story of bizarre murders and bizarre personalities." (Larson 1986, 84).

Another horror author puts the case for the book *Psycho* even more emphatically: "Almost every present-day writer of horror has in one way or another been influenced by *Psycho*. Call it a milestone in horror fiction, written by one of the greats. That's what it is and what he is."[11]

Psycho the Movie and Film Violence

It is ironic that both book and movie, modern classics of their kind, did not approach the detailed horror of the true story of Ed Gein. Yet the movie especially, while enhancing Alfred Hitchcock's international reputation as a director, is described as inspiring tasteless, graphic imitations that leave nothing to the imagination.[12] Bloch deplores the splatterfilms that have in turn inspired even more graphic details in horror literature in the trend categorized as splatterpunk. As he said in an interview in *Fear* magazine:

> I don't care for this particular trend because I feel it does a disservice to the field. It's very much analogous to the use of four letter words in contemporary fiction. These things are now buzz words: they've lost their impact. They're a substantive device for actual thought, and the same thing is true in a horror film visually. Anyone can eviscerate—or seem to eviscerate—on camera. It doesn't call for any skill or any imagination. . . . But this has nothing to do with the art or even the craft of the presentation of the fantastic, or the genuine horror film.[13]

Bloch explains the difference between more traditional horror and the new school that depicts more violence:

Another thing that has changed are the rules. People who have paid attention to my work and that of those who have been around for a while realize that we have been primarily writing morality plays. In this kind of fantasy we recognize good and evil, we make a value judgement, we generally have the good triumph, or if not there's a reason for it. We don't think anyone who has seen *Psycho* wants to grab a knife and go marching off in drag to pull shower curtains open. I don't think the character played by Tony Perkins led a particularly happy or rewarding life. A pitiable psychotic who comes to no good end. But today's antiheroes, with one justification, revenge, are then allowed to go out and perpetrate violence that is far more atrocious than that perpetrated upon themselves or their family or friends. There's no necessity for further plot development then to show them getting in and out of these situations. To me this is a cop-out and has nothing to do with the real horror film.[14]

Or, to sum it up more succinctly, Bloch has said, "There is a distinction to be made between that which inspires terror and that which inspires nausea" (Ross, 64).

Robert Bloch has written two sequels: *Psycho II* and *Psycho House*. Neither has the impact of the first title, for although they are written in his usual fine style, the real hooker is gone; we all know that Norman Bates is bats. The surprise is missing, except as Bloch tricks the reader into thinking falsely that Norman is the chief nut in *Psycho II*.

During Bloch's early growth as a writer, he did not limit himself to material that would be published in magazines and books. He also wrote scripts for radio dramas and later for television. His move to Hollywood in 1960 was prompted not by Hitchcock's purchase of movie rights to *Psycho* but by Bloch's own career direction. In fact Bloch did not write the screenplay for *Psycho* and, until the film's success, did not publicize the fact that he had written the original book. He has admitted that his perpetual association with the book has typecast him as a horror writer only, not a true description of his work, which has spread across a far-wider range of literature.

Once in Hollywood Bloch spent a great deal of time writing for television and the movies. Some of the scripts were based on his own work, such as *The Skull,* drawn from "The Skull of the Marquis de Sade." Some were based on the works of others, such as one of the scripts he novelized—*Twilight Zone, the Movie.* He continues to write in a variety of genres and today is one of the most respected authors in Hollywood. He has recently completed his autobiography.

Because of his career in both literature and film, Bloch is in a particularly strategic position to comment on the relationship between the two media. He says, "Today's films have set the standards—or the substandards—for both science fiction and horror, apparently acting on the precept that one good picture deserves five bad sequels. . . . So-called horror films are even worse [than science fiction]: they depend not only on special effects but on heavy-handed sex and violence that have little to do with story lines. . . . Taking their cues from this, many writers of horror fiction have sought to duplicate visual excesses with the written word; again, it's doubtful if they've managed to achieve anything except raise the speed level of a fast read."[15]

American Gothic

Another of Bloch's novels is also drawn from true crime—*American Gothic,* published in 1974. This novel is based on the appalling story of Herman Mudgett, alias Dr. H. H. Holmes, who in addition to being a bigamist committed a series of nauseating murders in Chicago nearly 100 years ago. As with Ed Gein and *Psycho,* the real story seems much more shocking than Bloch's account, inspired by the deeds of the amoral killer.

The man who was born Herman Webster Mudgett arrived in Chicago in the early 1890s after having had a series of shady careers elsewhere, including New England, Michigan, and Minnesota. Using the name H. H. Holmes he acquired a job in a drugstore, which he later bought from its owner, a Mrs. Holden. She disappeared mysteriously soon after. A very successful businessman, primarily in the area of hawking patent medicines and bogus cures, Mudgett/Holmes reputedly soon became wealthy. He built a castlelike home full of secret rooms and passageways and hired an attractive young woman, Julia Connor, and her husband. Julia's husband disappeared.[16]

Mudgett/Holmes diversified his business operations, hiring young women to help with the work. He preferred wealthy orphans. On a business trip to swindle money from prospective investors, he met Minnie Williams, who returned to Chicago with him. Once back home, Mudgett/Holmes quickly disposed of his Julia, now his mistress. An unknown number of other young women disappeared from Holmes's mansion. In time, Minnie too dropped out of sight. Later investigation would show that Mudgett/Holmes already had a number of wives scattered about the country.

With a collaborator, Mudgett/Holmes engaged in insurance fraud, which ultimately proved to be his undoing. When he was arrested, the Chicago authorities entered his mansion. There they discovered trapdoors, secret passages and chutes, gas chambers, and a windowless room lined with asbestos, as well as a crematorium, lime pits, and vats of acid. The villainous Mudgett/Holmes had carelessly left bloodstained clothing and fragments of human bones as evidence. He finally confessed to nearly 30 murders, and then later claimed 150, mostly young women. He was hanged in 1896 after cursing those who had caused his downfall.[17]

Bloch uses the Columbian World Exposition of 1893 as the colorful background in his Mudgett/Holmes story. The plot of *American Gothic* centers on Crystal Wilson, a female reporter assigned to cover the exposition (or world's fair, as it is called in the book) for her newspaper's women readers. Crystal is something of a feminist and, in the course of the book, discards her stodgy, conventional fiancé, Jim, for a co-worker, editor Charlie Hogan. Crystal also becomes fascinated with a pharmacist, G. Gordon Gregg, who the reader knows is not a nice person, since the first chapter describes his murder of his wife. Crystal almost becomes one of Gregg's victims in his mansion of murder, but she is saved, for a happy ending.

Randall D. Larson suggests Bloch has used the setting of the world's fair as a backdrop for a persistent theme of role-playing that occurs throughout *American Gothic*:

> Nearly every major character, at one point or another, imper-sonates the role of someone else for various reasons. Bloch pre-sents this theme in the very first chapter and with a most-appropriate subject: Gregg's castle itself, which of course isn't a real castle at all, only a sprawling three-story structure with a pharmacy below and rooms to rent above. It only *looks* like a castle. Millicent Gregg realizes that, just as she realizes that she, too, is playing a role. If the castle is not a real castle, then, neither is she the royal Lady she pretends to be, parading to join her husband in its phony splendor. . . .
>
> But the main roleplayer, of course, is Gregg himself. It is he who plays the friendly pharmacist, . . . the innocently accused businessman . . . the seductive romancer. . . . But these are only roles that Gregg plays, albeit with studied accomplish-ment. In reality, G. Gordon Gregg is a butcher who collects the hearts of women and keeps them in jars in his bedroom cabinet. (Larson 1986, 112)

Bloch reflects on role-playing and identity in an introduction to a collection of essays devoted to Stephen King: "I'm neither a phi-losopher nor a psychiatrist, and I must opt for the easy explana-tion. On the basis of personal belief and observation, I'd say those of us who direct our storytelling into darker channels do so be-cause we were perhaps a bit more mindful than most regarding our childhood confusions of identity, our conflicts with unpleas-ant realities and our traumatic encounters with imaginative terrors."[18]

Jack the Ripper

Bloch has obviously become an expert on true crime and the de-vious workings of the psychotic mind as a theme for scary stories. An early short story he wrote, "Yours Truly, Jack the Ripper," was about the elusive killer in London a century ago. The story still intrigues Bloch, who recently wrote:

> [Jack the Ripper's] trail of blood led nowhere, and to this day we do not know his name.
>
> Thus the Ripper remains as a symbol of all our secret fears—the fear of the stranger on a darkened street, fear of the neighbor whose commonplace exterior may conceal the beast within, even the fear of a friend we *think* we know; a friend who may become a fiend once the mask comes off and the knife comes out.[19]

Bloch's short story, written in 1943, is told by a Chicago psychiatrist, John Carmody. He is approached by Sir Guy Hollis, who tells him details about Jack the Ripper and says he believes the Ripper is at present in Chicago, although he should be dead of old age by this time. Carmody scoffs at the tale and at Hollis's evidence about the Ripper's present activities. Hollis believes the Ripper is like a vampire, able to live on the blood of those he slays. He says, "I tell you, a mad beast is loose on this world! An ageless, eternal beast, sacrificing to Hecate and the dark gods!"[20] The twist at the end, in Bloch's usual style, provides a proper shiver for the unsuspecting, for Carmody is the immortal Jack the Ripper, who raises a knife to kill Hollis in the story's final sentence.

The lack of graphic descriptions in "Jack the Ripper" is a Bloch trademark. Critics praise Bloch for his underplaying of gore and violence, depending instead on a jolt at the story's end to deliver the necessary wallop to the reader. As one states:

> Bloch's horror fiction also became distinctive for its restraint, in terms of graphic violence. While many of his early Lovecraftian stories described their terrors in ludicrous detail, his work subsequent to the '30s avoided this description completely. The gruesome murders that figured so prominently in "Yours Truly, Jack the Ripper," "Lizzie Borden Took an Axe," The House of the Hatchet" and others are never described outright. Rather, Bloch takes the occasion to shock us with a sudden punch-line, usually at the end of the story or chapter. . . . It's this restraint in story-telling which sets Bloch aside from many other horror

writers, particularly in the current vogue of graphic violence
and "splatter" horror in both films and literature.[21]

"Jack the Ripper" is one of Bloch's best known stories, and the
editors of a collection of Jack the Ripper tales say, "'Yours Truly,
Jack the Ripper' may be the most famous Ripper story ever written. Certainly it's the one that most people remember if you ask
them if they've ever read anything about Jack—and deservedly
so."[22] The story, written early in Bloch's career, is still in the Lovecraft style, offering a supernatural explanation for Jack. Bloch
continued his interest in the Whitechapel crimes through the
years and used the theme of the Ripper a number of times.

For example, another short story uses Jack as a character in a
different way. In "A Toy for Juliette" a spoiled beauty in the future
employs a sort of time machine to pluck historic figures from the
past to use as idle fancies. Her last toy, however, proves to be Jack
the Ripper, and Juliette's hobby suddenly becomes fatal.

Shortly before the Ripper's centennial, Bloch wrote a full-length
novel about Jack that explores the psychological makeup of various suspects before offering its own solution to the question, Who
was Jack the Ripper? Bloch's solution this time is clever and, if
true, helps explain why the crimes are still unsolved.[23] He suggests that a couple, a man and woman, acted together, thus dup-
ing the police, who were frantically searching for a single man. A
rather unsettling note is the woman, a nurse named Eva Sloane,
who reminds the reader a bit of *American Gothic*'s Crystal.

Bloch clearly understands the subtleties of horror and uses psychological factors to induce terror. In talking about Edgar Allan
Poe's masterpiece "The Tell-Tale Heart" Bloch said, "I think the
most horrifying thing that most people can imagine is persistence: something you can't stop, that inexorably continues. In
Poe's story—after all, conscience doth make cowards of us all—
the heart's beating was what forced the protagonist to confess.
Jack the Ripper captured that essence: When would these murders ever end? That's what scares us" (Larson 1986, 115).

In addition to understanding the nature of horror, Bloch uses
humor to good advantage. Larson points out examples of Bloch's

humor in the book *Night of the Ripper*: "Mark Robinson [the protagonist] alludes to a Michigan classmate of his named Herman Mudgett ('Now there was a cool one for you—he could carve up a cadaver with a dull butter knife and never turn a hair . . . he's probably enjoying a brilliant career as a surgeon right now')".[24] Larson goes on to say, "This extension of the Ripper's violence into ourselves—we all are capable of horrendous acts, to one extent or another—is the real theme of *The Night of the Ripper*. Dr. Trebor [a colleague] remarks on this very fact, correlating a performance of *Dr. Jekyll and Mr. Hyde* with the abrupt psychological changes capable in many people: '. . . suppose there's something inside the brain itself that can sometimes be summoned to take control. Perhaps we all have a monster hidden inside us' [ch. 8]. Trebor's sentiment recalls Norman Bates's remark in *Psycho* that 'we all go a little crazy' at times" (Larson 1986, 116).

In *Night of the Ripper* Bloch does not resort to a supernatural explanation for the solution to the Jack the Ripper crimes. By now a recognized international authority on Jack the Ripper, he admits in an author's note there is no complacency on his part that the notorious killer must be dead by now: "It would be comforting to believe that this sort of activity [the murders] came to an end in 1888, but such a conclusion is difficult to accept. And while the author is fully accountable for any imaginary violence in these pages he is, regrettably, not responsible for the nightly news."[25]

Grisly reminders of history's repeated inhumanities are used as epigrams to the chapters in *The Night of the Ripper*. Any reader wanting graphic examples of horrible crimes need only read these short descriptions. Reality is often much worse than fictional imagination, a fact Bloch uses skillfully in his writing.

Bloch is an accomplished and thoroughly professional author. Although he has written in various genres, including mainstream fiction, he recognizes the universal delight in horror as a fascination for readers, including teens:

> One of the lures of horror fiction is a constant in the human race—curiosity. It's not fashionable today to speak about emo-

tions except in a knowledgeable way. To confess that one is naïve is taboo. But I think that today's youngsters are not much different from those of any previous generation in that they are curious about death and its mysteries, about physiological and psychological symptoms. And the mere fact that it is *verboten* to discuss such matters in ordinary conversation causes them to be even more interested. . . .

As long as human beings experience fear, horror will be a timeless emotion. I can scarcely visualize the human being who doesn't have fear, whether it's expressed or secret. (Winter 1985, 22.)

8. A Pause for Splatterpunk

A new trend in horror fiction became sufficiently evident during the 1980s for most people to notice, for some to complain, and for the new subgenre to be given a name: splatterpunk.

The term *splatterpunk* was coined in 1984 by David J. Schow, one of the new, younger breed of horror writers who depict a violent, sexually explicit world. As a school of writing, splatterpunk is hard precisely to identify and circumscribe because writers who are described as typical of the subgenre in one source may well deny being part of splatterpunk in another source. The subgenre is young both in its definition and in its practitioners. No one knows whether it is a strong trend that will continue or is one that will attract attention only briefly before dwindling away.

Although some of the older, more established horror writers, such as Robert Bloch, protest the excesses of splatterpunk (which leave little to the imagination), other writers see the trend as a sure sign that horror literature is maturing and growing: "There's no surer sign that a type of fiction has come of age than when its youngest writers begin to rebel against its conventions. More than 20 years after horror fiction made a clean break with its pulp heritage, learned some manners, moved into a neighborhood near you under the name of 'dark fantasy' and began acting like mainstream literature, its newest generation of authors has refused to uphold the traditions established by their elders."[1]

Ray Garton, a younger author of such books as *Live Girls, Crucifax Autumn,* and *Lot Lizard,* describes the start of splatterpunk:

> I was at the convention where that term was born, and it was done as a joke because a bunch of younger writers were not getting along with some of the older school of horror writers. So in order to separate themselves, they came up with this term "splatterpunk" and joked about making it a whole movement. Well, it wasn't long before it became a whole movement and magazines were doing articles on it. I don't like being included in that group for a couple of reasons. I think that sort of fiction defeats the purpose of horror; splatterpunk books aren't morality plays like most horror—which is the way I think horror should be. The other reason is I don't want to be associated with any group. I'm already having problems with the label "horror writer." It's not that I mind being called a "horror writer"—because I started out writing horror and I enjoy reading it—as long as I'm allowed to write something else once in a while.[2]

David Schow, author of *The Kill Riff,* defends the movement:

> Splatterpunk came about as a term . . . for a style of horror that is loud, sometimes uncultured, not without literary merit, but doesn't eschew gory special effects, written by people who were nurtured by the horror films of the Seventies, Rock and roll—that whole cultural mulch: Vietnam, *The Untouchables,* Television Will Kill Your Children—that whole upbringing we all had. It's heavily influenced by music and movies and television and videos in a way that earmarks it as being different from the gothic, baroque, extremely literary and academic type of horror writing.[3]

Such debate on the direction of a field of literature is healthy. It shows that there is growth in the area, that some writers want to stretch the existing boundaries of the genre. Without experimentation and challenge a genre can become boring. When that happens the writing often becomes moribund, people stop reading it, and publishers stop publishing it. Splatterpunk has been commended for its raw power: "For all its noise and occasional sloppiness, splatterpunk has an energy often noticeably lacking in competently executed dark fantasy" (Dziemianowicz, 96).

Nastiness and Violence

It is possible to draw parallels between the splatterpunk movement in the United States and the "nasty" school in Great Britain. During the 1970s a number of British writers, such as James Herbert and Shaun Hutson, wrote books about animal mutations that went around terrorizing people—for instance, giant rats and slugs. These authors were criticized for their comic-book approach to writing and their direct, graphic violence. Clive Barker was lumped into the nasty school a bit later: he is sometimes cited as an influential person in the splatterpunk movement, occasionally being called "The Father of Splatterpunk," a title he seems to dislike.

Another parallel with the debate over splatterpunk is the continuing controversy about violence in the movies. John Russo, a writer for the film *Night of the Living Dead*—which contributed to the growing use of blood and gore in the 1970s and 1980s— commented in *Newsweek* magazine, "These films *are* horrifying because they reflect—but do not create—a frightful trend in our society. Murders, assaults and rapes are being committed with more frequency and with increasing brutality. Serial killers and mass murderers are constantly making headlines. Most of these killers are men, often sexually warped men, and they most often kill women. So we filmmakers have stuck to the facts in our portrayal of them. That's why our movies are so scary. Too many of our fellow citizens are turning into monsters, and contemporary horror movies have seized upon this fear and personified it."[4]

Some Misgivings

Another younger American writer sometimes classed with the violent school of writing is Richard Christian Matheson, son of the highly revered fantasy/horror writer Richard Matheson. R. C. Matheson's specialty to date has been short, powerful stories, some of which have been collected into *Scars,* published in 1988. In response to a question regarding his "membership" in the Splat Pack, he replied, "I don't really subscribe to that approach to horror fiction. I'm much more psychologically inclined. It's the stuff that you can't see that's a lot more interesting. So how on earth I ever got into that I have no idea. . . . It clearly is not my approach. In *Penthouse* I said if their approach was the knife that opens the vein, mine is the needle that injects the virus."[5]

It might seem that more people are eager *not* to be classified as splatterpunk than are willing to be placed in that grouping. Even those writers who seem happy to be in the group confess to occasional lapses of inhibition—as John Skipp does here: "All the traditional taboos—incest, bestiality, cannibalism—have become the fodder of horror and only new father John Skipp confessed to one occasion of self-censorship. 'There was an opportunity in our current novel for baby killing and I really had to back off from it,' John admits, 'but you sometimes have to write things that you would otherwise balk at, instances where anything else would be cheating'" (Horsting, 34).

Splatterpunk has been compared with the cyberpunk movement in science fiction. It is a harsh, gritty, urban scene full of weird punk people involved in unsavory activities. Music, drink, and drugs are often found in splatterpunk, and sexual morality of any sort is missing. The protagonists are usually young—some are teenagers—groping for sense in a modern world gone mad. Even the most sheltered reader cannot deny that the world has changed and that splatterpunk may well be no worse than a reality we may not want to face.

One book that can be examined more closely as an example of splatterpunk is Ray Garton's *Crucifax Autumn,* which was censored during the editing process. It was purchased by Pocket Books, which published it in 1988. Garton describes this work:

> It's about a bunch of directionless teenagers in the San Fernando Valley who fall under the spell of a sort of MTV-type Pied Piper of the Eighties. He leads them into an underworld of drugs and sex . . . my God, I'm talking like cover copy . . . he leads them into this world of drugs and sex and crime while their parents are sitting around scratching their heads going, "What's happening to our kids? It's the rock 'n' roll! It's the sex in the movies! It's drugs!" And both the parents and religious organizations begin pointing their fingers at symptoms rather than at causes.[6]

Included in the story is Nikki's grotesque abortion by Mace, the charismatic villain. Repulsive yet riveting, the scene was originally cut by the editors:

> When I was told the abortion scene had to go, the reason given was that it didn't work and was "simply too much." I didn't understand. *I* thought it worked, of course, and since this was a horror novel and not a romantic comedy, I didn't understand the "it's simply too much" reason. I pressed it a little, confident that the editor would change her mind. But she didn't.
>
> I kept asking for a better reason to cut a whole scene like that—a fairly big scene—and all I got was that it was too horrible and that to perform an abortion with a tongue was physically impossible. This was backed up by my editor's assistant. When I asked them if they were troubled by the fact that Mace had a three foot tongue and they said no, I reminded them that it was physically impossible for a guy to *have* a three foot tongue and that one of the elements frequently involved in horror novels was a certain amount of fantasy and suspension of belief, and with all of that in mind, why was it such a big deal to perform an abortion with a tongue if it *fit*. They were immovable. I was astonished. That was when they agreed to let me water down the scene rather than cut it altogether if that would make me feel better.[7]

Even watered-down, the rewritten scene of Nikki's abortion holds the reader's attention with shock as Nikki's friends Jeff and Lily watch with awe and growing horror:

The tongue slid down over her belly, leaving a sparkling trail like an oversized slug.

"—thou annointest my head with oil—"

It eased lower still, over her navel, toward the triangle of hair between her legs . . .

"—my cup runneth over; surely g-goodness and m-mercy—"

Jeff's guts chilled as Mace's tongue continued its descent. . . .

"Holy Jesus," he whispered, turning to Lily and pulling her away from the hole, somehow certain of what was about to happen. Open-mouthed and breathless, Lily resisted at first, but he jerked her hard into his trembling arms and pressed her face to his shoulder, whispering into her ear, "Don't watch, Lily, d-don't look at this. . . ."

Jeff heard a deep moan of pleasure catch in Nikki's throat and turn into a cough.

Soft wet sounds—moist sliding sounds—were buried by the reverend's gibbering voice: "Oh, God, don't do this, dear Jesus, merciful Father in heaven, *don't do this!*"

Jeff felt lightheaded as he closed his eyes and held Lily tight; he felt as if he had somehow tripped and fallen into someone else's nightmare as Nikki began to make dry, pained retching sounds.

"Nikki?" Lily whispered.

Jeff pressed her face harder to his shoulder. His jaws ached from clenching his teeth.

Nikki screamed. It was unlike any scream Jeff had ever heard; it tore from her lungs like skin from bone.[8]

The scene in its bowdlerized version ends with the minister fainting, Jeff and Lily fleeing, and Nikki vomiting. In the original version the scene continues, with a descriptive passage of Mace's eating the fetus.

When asked if this experience with censorship had made him more cautious as a writer, Garton responded:

> I do consciously censor myself, but not as a result of my *Crucifax* experience. It's more as a result of the Splatterpunk movement, in which I have so often been included. In fact, I *welcomed* the inclusion at first, but then took a few steps back and thought about it a little. I began to think that a lot of writers—myself included—were throwing in a lot of graphic sex and violence just for the hell of it, just to outdo their last book,

or somebody *else's* book and it was getting pretty disgusting. Plus it was resulting in some pretty poor storytelling. (Gauntlet, 29)

More Violence

Part of splatterpunk's appeal—or revulsion, depending on the reader's outlook—lies in the often-lengthy descriptive passages of what really happens to flesh and blood. For example, when Rudy, the vampire in John Skipp and Craig Spector's *The Light at the End,* is exposed to sunlight,

> it began with the x-shaped brand at the base of the skull, the blistering bald spot at the crown: a mottled, red-black scum oozed up to the surface as if squeezed from a tube. It slopped over his shoulders and down the sides of his head as he jerked and stiffened like a man being pulled apart by horses. His head lolled back, face contorted with agony. Sunlight hit the cross-hatched tattoo across the broken nose, the sore on the lip, the dangling earlobe. A pale slime, like blood and blobs of curdled milk, spilled down into his open mouth.[9]

As coauthor Skipp tells of the writing, "We fired every megawatt of juice we had into that thing. It was sort of like the sessions at Termite Terrace must have been, where the great Warner Bros. cartoons of the thirties and forties were done. We just kept thinking of the wildest, most terrible things; and the worst it got, the more jazzed we got. I think it was that enthusiasm, and the fact that we *went for it,* that accounts for the book's appeal. They just hadn't seen a novel that was quite so unrelentingly, jubilantly *overt.*"[10]

One commentator on *The Light at the End* said, "At first it looked like just another trashy terror book. But it sure didn't read like one. It had a style all of its own and co-authored voice that refused to speak politely: it shouted, and the prose, though often overwrought, was never boring, never safe. It was gory, it was violent, sometimes it was downright painful. But it had heart and soul and characters for whom you could care. It got some good reviews, it got some bad. But ultimately, it sold."[11]

The future of the splatterpunk movement seems uncertain without more authors acknowledging its worth; at this point it seems to have lost momentum. Some writers, like Ray Garton, have left the splatterpunk fold. Even David J. Schow, who remains faithful to the movement, admits that it's not an easy style to write in, as he explains about a new book he's recently finished, *The Shaft*: "*The Shaft* was excruciating to write because it's such a bleak book and when you have to crawl inside that environment to steep yourself in the mood you want to convey it becomes highly oppressive. This book is peopled with fucked-up lives and that's tough to live with for any length of time, so I had periodically to leave it to work on other things just so I didn't get depressed."[12]

Schow's characters may be depressing, both to him and his growing band of readers, but they are real people. As Charles de Lint says, "You might not like a lot of them [the characters in Schow's book, *The Kill Riff*], but you *believe* in them. The backgrounds of the L. A. rock music and advertising scenes are perfectly brought to life. The action, when the story's in an action mode, moves like a locomotive, but there's also time for insightful explorations of the human psyche which show that Schow has a real grasp of what makes people the way they are. And those quieter moments in no way slow the story down.[13]

Schow does not write only brutal splatterpunk; he is capable of far more delicate fiction as well. As he describes his approach to writing short stories, "Basically I like to keep one hand right over your heart, with the other one poised to rip your intestines out and strangle you with them, as a fallback. On the one hand, you have 'Pamela's Get,' the kind of story which is from the heart; on the other hand, you have the story I'm currently finishing for the *Book of the Dead* project [edited by Skipp and Spector], which is called 'Jerry's Kids Meet Wormboy' and is about as subtle as being slapped in the face with your own bladder" (de Lint, 28).

At present only a few writers wish to be called splatterpunk authors—and understandably so, for it is limiting to be classified. Authors should be free to write what they want, not be forced by a demanding public into a narrow school of writing. The splatter-punk philosophy can be credited with making a valid case for itself, although as a subgenre it may not appeal to many writers and readers. It can be criticized for grossness but cannot be faulted for lack of honesty. Its very harshness is part of our society today, a society that has come about not because of planning and desires but because it has evolved with flaws as well as some successes. Only by considering what is wrong can we attempt to change things for the better.

9. The King of Dark Fantasy: Stephen King and Teens

One of the best-known authors writing today is Stephen King. He is popular with adults and teens, and a number of his works have been made into movies. A relatively young man, barely into his middle years, King grew up in the generation following World War II. A tradition of American horror literature had been established, although it was definitely not mainstream literature. Stephen King found it, and millions of his readers have been the happier for his discovery, including many who are not ordinarily frequent readers of horror fiction.

Like other kids of his generation, King as a youth was inspired by E. C. Comics (which in turn inspired his *Creepshow* movies) and by the wonderful black-and-white B movies that were shown in movie theaters across America in the middle years of this century. King has also paid tribute to authors who influenced him, among them Ira Levin, Richard Matheson, and Robert Bloch, "the writers who seem to generate the most raw, sweaty-palmed suspense in me."[1] King writes in the tradition of dark fantasy, and although his books are usually classified as horror literature, only some of his themes involve supernatural elements. In his early books especially, King turned to psychic phenomena, as well as supernatural ideas, to create terror of the unknown in his popular stories.

Stephen King is commonly regarded as a publishing phenomenon. Certainly he is what is sometimes called a brand-name author, one whose works are bought by faithful readers solely because they were written by that person. King's popularity can be illustrated by the frequency with which his books appear on the best-seller lists, both in original hardcover and in paperback-reprint versions. He is an author whose works and peripheral materials are collected by many as an investment, and special editions of his books—including a limited edition of *Firestarter* that contains an asbestos cover—are published often. King has many loyal fans, including teenagers, who read his books and stories avidly.

Stephen King: Is He Really the Best of All?

> But because I am a horror novelist and also a child of my times, and because I believe that horror does not horrify unless the reader or viewer has been personally touched, you will find the autobiographical element constantly creeping in. Horror in real life is an emotion that one grapples with . . . all alone. It is a combat waged in the secret recesses of the heart.[2]
>
> —Stephen King

Much has been written by and about Stephen King. As a writer of popular books he has been most sharing of his time and thoughts with interviewers, critics, and other writers. His great success in recent years has led him to guard his privacy carefully, but one can sense from secondhand sources that King is a friendly kind of guy. In speaking of fame he has said, "Being famous sucks. There is no upside. The downside is when you realize that the only reason everything on the buffet is free is because they're planning on having you for dessert" (*Mystery Scene*, 5).

Stephen King was born in Maine, where he lives today. His father, a merchant seaman, deserted the family when Steve was only two, and his mother, Nellie, turned to a series of menial jobs to support her two sons. Nellie was a caring mother, and although money may have been in short supply in the King home, love was

Chronology: Stephen King's Life and Works

1948 Stephen Edwin King born 21 September in Portland, Maine, the second son of Nellie Pillsbury King and Donald King, a merchant sailor.

1949 Donald King deserts the family, and Nellie King works to support her children, in various locations in New England and the Midwest.

1958 The King family moves to Durham, Maine, where Nellie cares for her aging parents. Stephen discovers his father's old paperback books and starts writing horror fiction.

1965 First published story, "I Was a Teenage Grave Robber."

1966 Graduates from Lisbon Falls High School.

1967 First professional story, "The Glass Floor," published in *Startling Mystery Stories*.

1970 Graduates from the University of Maine, Orono, with a major in English.

1971 Marries Tabitha Spruce; they later have three children: Naomi, Owen, and Joe.

1974 *Carrie.*

1975 *'Salem's Lot.*

1976 Film version of *Carrie* released.

1977 *Rage* (using Bachman pseudonym) and *The Shining.*

1978 *The Stand* and *Night Shift.*

1979 *The Dead Zone* and *The Long Walk* (Bachman). Television version of *'Salem's Lot* shown.

1980 Moves to present home in Bangor, Maine. Three best-sellers appear simultaneously on list: *Firestarter, The Dead Zone,* and *The Shining.* Film version of *The Shining* released.

1981 *Cujo, Danse Macabre,* and *Roadwork* (Bachman).

1982 *The Dark Tower: The Gunslinger, Different Seasons, Creepshow,* and *The Running Man* (Bachman). Film version of *Creepshow* released.

1983 *Christine, Pet Sematary,* and *Cycle of the Werewolf.* Film versions of *Cujo, The Dead Zone* and *Christine* released.

1984 *The Talisman* (with Peter Straub), *The Eyes of the Dragon,* and *Thinner* (Bachman). Films *Children of the Corn, Cat's Eye,* and *Firestarter* released.

1985 *Castle Rock: The Stephen King Newsletter* commences publication. *Skeleton Crew.* Film *Silver Bullet* released.

1986 *Misery* and *It.* Films *Maximum Overdrive* and *Stand by Me* released.

1987 *The Tommyknockers.* Film *Creepshow II* and film version of *The Running Man* released.

1989 *The Darker Half.* Film version of *Pet Sematary* released.

not. King's recollections of his childhood reflect a normal boyhood, except for the absence of his father. One important episode stands out in his memory—discovering a box of horror books that had belonged to his father and finding out that his father had been an aspiring writer. Stephen King started to write at an early age, determining early that he wanted to have a career as an author.

In an interview with Douglas Winter, King was asked if he felt alienated and read a great deal as a kid. He responded:

> Only to a degree. Inside, I felt different and unhappy a lot of times. I felt *violent* a lot of times. . . .
> But I hung out with the kids. I worked on cars, played sports as much as I could. . . . I had to play football, because I was big. If you didn't play football and you were big, it meant you were a fucking faggot, right? That's what it's like when you come from a small town.[3]

After graduating from Lisbon Falls High School, King attended the University of Maine, where he majored in English, wrote for the school newspaper (a column entitled "King's Garbage Truck"), and met his wife-to-be, Tabitha Spruce. He continued to write, publishing his first professional story, "The Glass Floor," in *Startling Mystery Stories* in fall 1967. During his college years he also wrote books that would later be published under the name Richard Bachman, including *Rage* and *The Long Walk*. King graduated from college in 1970 and married Tabitha Spruce a year later.

The struggling young couple worked at various jobs, including one in a laundry. While teaching high school at Hampton Academy, King made his first big breakthrough: an editor at Doubleday, Bill Thompson, bought *Carrie*. The book sold well, particularly in paperback, and King was on his way. Additional books were written and published, and by the beginning of the 1980s King was a best-selling author. Movies were made of his books; his pseudonym, Richard Bachman, was revealed; and the name Stephen King became a household word, or, as his biographer, Douglas Winter, puts it, "Stephen King's reign of terror had begun."[4]

Since that time Stephen King has become a famous and wealthy writer. His stories are in demand for movies and television, and collectors avidly buy anything connected with him. His own newsletter, *Castle Rock,* ran successfully for some years, and he even bought his own radio station, which plays his favorite rock-and-roll music.

King's Teenage Characters

King as a youth had determined he wanted a career as an author, and he was wise enough to write about the things he knew as a teenager. Being male, he usually wrote about young men and their feelings, although his first big professional success was about a teenage girl. King has created many believable characters, and some of the most memorable have been teens.

One of the youngest Stephen King teens is Gordie Lachance, a 12-year-old kid who later becomes a writer. The reader cannot help but think King is writing about himself at this age as he describes the overnight trip Gordie and his three friends take to see a corpse in the woods. "The Body" is the autumn section in *Different Seasons* and was made into the excellent film *Stand by Me,* directed by Rob Reiner. The four boys in both the story and the film are exuberant, curious kids, highly believable in their desire to see what a dead person their own age looks like. One of the highlights of both story and film occurs when the young storyteller Gordie shares a wonderful tale he has concocted about the revenge of a fat kid, Lard Ass Hogan. King admits to identifying with characters like Lard Ass, people who are forced to react in violent ways.[5]

King's sympathy for the misfit, the outsider, comes through time and time again in his stories. He has obviously never forgotten those feelings of isolation and alienation which are so common during the teenage years, and he describes these emotions with

sympathy and understanding. He offers no quick solutions for as-
suaging these feelings, for we know there are none. Here is one
of the clues to Stephen King's popularity as an author with teens;
he remembers what adolescence was like and tells about it with
honesty.

In one of his short stories, "Word Processor of the Gods," King
describes two other teens, cousins as dissimilar as can be. Seen
through the eyes of an adult, they are almost personifications of
evil and good. Seth, at 15, is the sullen and despised son of the
protagonist. Jon, a bit younger, is a bright and engaging young
electronics genius. When Jon and his parents are killed in a car
accident, his uncle receives the word processor Jon had jerry-built
from odds and ends. The new owner discovers to his delight and
fascination that the word processor will grant his wishes, and so
he first deletes his own son and wife and then replaces them with
Jon and his mother to create an idyllic new family.

"Apt Pupil"

Another story in *Different Seasons* tells of a teenager just slightly
older than Gordie. This is Todd Bowden, the 13-year-old protagonist of "Apt Pupil," the summer section of the book. Todd is not
as sympathetic and likable as Gordie, but King gets inside the
character and takes the reader on a frightening path that leads
to Todd's disintegration.

At the beginning of the story Todd is shown to be a bright,
healthy, attractive youngster. In the early days of his summer
vacation, however, he discovers that a neighbor is a former officer
of a German concentration camp. Threatening to reveal the old
man's secret, Todd blackmails the German into telling about his
experiences, particularly scenes of horror and torture. Todd's fascination for the details of this terrible time becomes obsessive,
and for the next few years he dwells on Nazi terrorism. Then Todd
starts to kill. The seemingly wholesome young man is, by the age
of 17, as corrupt as his mentor.

In addition to being known as a brand-name author, King is
associated with brand names in a different way, one that "Apt

Pupil" well illustrates. Especially in his earlier books, King often refers to commercial products and celebrities, thereby producing a small jolt of recognition in the reader. As Robert R. Harris has observed:

> In the novella "Apt Pupil," Mr. King pulls out all stops. Here is a partial list of the brand (and other) names that appear in that short work: Schwinn, Nike, Timex, A-1 Steak Sauce, Motorola, "Real People," National Geographic, Kools, Keds, Kodak, Johnny Carson, Hall's Mentho-lyptus, Valium, Architectural Digest, Robert Ludlum, Lawrence Welk, Hyatt, Porsche, Scotch tape, Ring Dings, "Hogan's Heroes," Coke, Diamond Blue-Tip matches, Krazy Glue, "The Flintstones," Shell No-Pest Strip, Big Macs, Penthouse, Revlon, *Reader's Digest,* Wildroot Cream Oil, Budweiser, Lawn-Boy, HBO, I.B.M., Hush Puppies, Smokenders and (ah! the ominous) Winchester.
>
> The cumulative effect of this piling on of names is to make the reader feel at home in this story about an ex-Nazi with a penchant for butchering winos and the all-American teen-age boy who becomes his accomplice. At a crucial moment in the story, the teen-ager must help the ex-Nazi hide a body and clean up his kitchen after a particularly bloody murder before the authorities arrive. "Where's your cleaner? Lestoil . . . Top Job," the boy asks. Never mind that in writing such a hilariously deflating line Mr. King is being absolutely sincere. Just imagine the shocked reader thinking, "Oh my God, I use Lestoil." It is the kind of reader identification that endears Mr. King to his fans.[6]

The Long Walk

In one of his Bachman novels, *The Long Walk,* King tells the story of 16-year-old Ray Garraty in a future society. In this world there is a deadly new contest in which walkers begin a trek from the U.S.–Canadian border across Maine toward Boston. Rules are strict and no sleep or rest is permitted. The walkers keep going until only one is left. Dropouts are instantly killed, but because the lone winner receives a fabulous prize, contestants are always available.

Ray is a bit vague as to why he decides to go on the long walk; once he has started, however, he refuses to quit. He walks with great determination as others drop around him, until the end, when he is the only one left. Then Ray starts to run.

Carrie

Carrie, immortalized in King's novel of the same name, is a teenage girl so naive that she is terrified when her first menstrual period starts in gym class. She has no idea what it all means. Most of the other girls are cruel and taunt her. Carrie gets no aid or comfort at home from her mother, a religious fanatic. One girl in Carrie's class, Sue, feels pity for the odd teen and befriends her, but all ends in disaster when Carrie, having been deliberately befouled by a bucketful of pig's blood at the prom, turns her ESP powers to revenge. The teens at the dance all perish as Carrie sets the school on fire with her telekinetic talents. To complete her retaliation against those who have been mean to her, Carrie returns home to confront her mother in a final scene of death and disaster. Although the outcome is certainly extreme, teens can relate to Carrie's feelings and secretly delight in her response. As the introduction to *The Gothic World of Stephen King* suggests, "The teenager loves to read King. . . . The King child protagonist addresses the problems of the child reader. Carrie White, for example, is a 'nerd' who is teased at school by her peers and tormented at home by a fanatic mother, situations no doubt experienced by a number of teenage readers."[7]

This idea is also explored by Thomas Monteleone, a young horror writer who admires King's ability to depict teenagers in a gripping and truthful way while still giving these characters a chance to strike back:

> When we see the world through the eyes of a Carrie White or an Arnie Cunningham [*Christine*], we are suddenly aware of how terribly cruel and heartless adolescent life can be: the callous denial of friendship and companionship often brought on by real or imagined differences that will seem so trivial in

adulthood. Letting us inside the heads of the ugly ducklings is effective, to be sure, but King takes things one step farther. He allows us to share in the satisfaction of striking back, the inevitable *revenge* which comes gushing out in response to the pain and punishment endured by his sympathetic protagonists. Within the reader, this catharsis may evoke past injustices that still cry out to be avenged, further enhancing strong identification with King's characters. This primal, loss-of-innocence kind of vengeance has a timeless, almost classic appeal, especially when its landscape is defined by the boundaries of the American high school and populated by the archetypal figures of every high school class in the country.[8]

The universal appeal of *Carrie* was apparent to viewers in the fine movie based on the book and directed by Brian De Palma. A later musical based on the book was a flop, however, showing that as a rule we like musicals to have more upbeat endings. In fact although there are elements of the Cinderella fairy tale in *Carrie* (until its savage end), it is a sombre folk tale. As Chelsea Quinn Yarbro wryly remarks, "[Carrie] will have to give back Prince Charming, who is not truly her own."[9] There is an almost-inevitable march toward doom in *Carrie*, but that is what we often like in horror literature. In fact the end of *Carrie* seems foreordained: "Because she is such a doomed victim, King makes Carrie's destruction of school and town seem more like an unconscious reaction than purposeful revenge, practically as impossible to prevent as the conditions which provoked it."[10]

Christine

Despite its touches of King's humor, *Christine* is not a funny book. It is sometimes referred to as the teenage boy's counterpart to *Carrie,* for it tells the story of a doomed young man, Arnie Cunningham (no relation to the family on television's "Happy Days"), and his love affair with a car, Christine. Arnie, at 17, is a typical nerd. His only real friend is Dennis, a sincere athlete. Arnie is an outsider at school; however, when he sees the old wreck of a 1958

Plymouth Fury, it's love at first sight, and Arnie no longer cares about his social situation at school, for he has Christine, his car.

Arnie carefully reconstructs Christine and in so doing becomes more personable. He acquires a girlfriend, Leigh, who, like Dennis, senses from the beginning that Christine is evil. But Arnie will heed no one's cautions about his beloved car, for Christine is fiercely loyal to Arnie as it/she eliminates Arnie's enemies one by one. Dennis and Leigh finally try to destroy Christine and think they succeed, despite the car's ability to repair itself. Then Arnie is killed in a car accident with his mother, and Dennis, years later, is left wondering whether Christine has truly been eliminated after all.

On one level *Christine* is a story of adolescent coming-of-age. Christine can be anthropomorphized into an "older woman" of 21, the femme fatale who fascinates Arnie and leads him to his destruction. On another level, however, as suggested by Linda C. Badley,

> *Christine* is about a cultural midlife crisis that re-enacts adolescence; it is also about adolescence as a self-perpetuating cycle. The novel reflects not one but at least two generations of middle-aged adolescents. One is King's age and is reliving the past; the other, younger, but more self-consciously "punk" generation consists of rebels without causes who have too many vehicles, who are all dressed up with no place to go. In so doing, it suggested an intimate relationship between the timeless (or is it haunted?) world of adolescence and our contemporary American way of life. In Dennis's nightmares, years after the events of the main story have taken place, Christine appears wearing a vanity plate, a "grinning white skull on a dead black field" and imprinted with the words, "ROCK 'N ROLL WILL NEVER DIE."[13]

Christine, the car with some kind of supernatural power, is basically evil. The origin, like that of the evil of the vehicles in the short story "Trucks," is never really explained—it's just there, and it's bad.

For teens, a likable element in *Christine* is King's constant references to music. Music is important to adolescents, and recognition of this fact is yet another reason that King's fiction is so popular among teens. The music in *Christine* is also a powerful force in the movie based on the book, because the throbbing beat of the songs help create the same feeling of impending doom that made *Carrie* so successful.

"The Raft"

A final example of King's use of teens as protagonists is the 19-year-old college students in the short story "The Raft," a piece also used in the movie *Creepshow II*. In this story two couples head for an isolated lake on what will probably be the last warm day of autumn. On reaching the lake they swim to an anchored raft, noticing when they arrive that there is an odd patch of dark "something" floating on the water near the raft. The "something" turns out to be an unknown substance that oozes around the raft and eventually eats the four young people. Along the way, the reader finds out something about the character and moral fiber of these four—a chilling exploration, because they are not very sympathetic people. Yet the reader is forced to fear with them and feel the need for self-preservation rising. The story forces the reader to ask, What would I do in this situation?

Although "The Raft" is a short piece, the story, according to William F. Nolan, is significant: "Here King is relentless and unsparing. The graphic description of one teenager's bloody demise, as he is sucked to bone-grinding death through a between-boards crack in the raft, is brilliantly revolting—the ultimate King gross-out."[14]

Michael R. Collings suggests yet another dimension to this story—the idea that sexual intercourse is a threat to the characters. Indeed, it proves to be the undoing of Randy (could King have named this character tongue-in-cheek?) and LaVerne, who have sex on the raft after a night of watchful terror. Immediately following, the bloblike substance gets into LaVerne's hair and consumes her as Randy watches in horror, so immobilized that he loses his one chance to escape by swimming to shore while the blob is busy eating LaVerne.[15]

Another key to King's popularity is his ability to delineate well-drawn characters. In fact, as he told Douglas Winter, he believes character to be the essential element of a good horror story: "You have got to love the people. See, that's the real paradox. There has to be love involved, because the more you love . . . then that allows horror to be possible. There is no horror without feeling" (*TZ*, 22). King admits to having problems depicting nonstereotypical women and minorities. Nevertheless, in his books he has created a number of people whom teens like to read about, including teenagers like themselves.

Violence and Humor

From the beginning King had to deal with criticism of his graphic violence, an element called the gross-out. He explains, "On top is the 'gross-out' level—when Regan vomits in the priest's face or masturbates with a crucifix in *The Exorcist*, or when the raw-looking, terribly inside-out monster in John Frankenheimer's *Prophecy* crunches off the helicopter pilot's head like a Tootsie-Pop. The gross-out can be done with varying degrees of artistic finesse, but it's always there" (*Macabre*, 17).

Yet King's use of the gross-out is carefully balanced with other emotions. Readers may still be gasping in shock over a particularly gruesome description when they are presented with something that makes them laugh. One critic on the humor in "The Body" says that work "is laced with a wild gallows humor which at times approaches celebratory glee."[11] Or, as Richard Bleiler, noted authority on supernatural fiction, describes King's humor, "King is a witty writer; his recent works often contain subtle and humorous allusions to his earlier novels, as well as many quietly sly jokes that are never belabored. Even evil is not immune to King's humor. The first words of Randall Flagg, the evil force in

The Stand (1978), after he yells to see if a starving Lloyd Henreid will respond, are from Maurice Sendak's children's book *Where the Wild Things Are*. They provide an amusing connection between Sendak's title and Flagg's location—a maximum-security prison."[12]

King's humor is evident even in short little phrases, such as his description in *Christine* of a garage office as "Early American Carburetor" and, later in that book, his remark that pre-Christmas rush "book reports were turned in late and often bore a suspicious resemblance to jacket copy (after all, how many sophomore English students are apt to call *The Catcher in the Rye,* 'this burning classic of postwar adolescence?')".

Psychic Phenomena

Part of the appeal of horror stories lies in people's fear of the unknown. To give this scary touch, traditional dark fantasy employs supernatural elements. And although King does use the supernatural in some of his stories, he has also made considerable use of another unknown—psychic phenomena.

Psychic phenomena, often referred to as ESP (extrasensory perception), include a number of occurrences that cannot be explained but have been under scientific investigation for the past century. Such investigation has entailed searching haunted houses, raising the spirits of the dead, levitation, astral projection, clairvoyance, psychokinesis, and second sight, among other methods. Although there has been considerable discussion and debunking by skeptics, the actual existence of these supposed powers of extrasensory perception has never been proved or disproved. Those who have experienced anything resembling a psychic experience, even a simple case of déjà vu, tend to believe that such things may be possible. The skeptics, on the other hand, insist that no psychic phenomena exist and claim that the so-called scientific investigations of these occurrences employ flawed methodologies and are prone to be perpetrated by hucksters and frauds.

When asked about paranormal abilities, King once responded, "I wouldn't say I believe in [it]. The scientific verdict's still out on most of those things, and they're certainly nothing to accept as an article of faith. But I don't think we should dismiss them out of hand just because we can't as yet understand how and why they operate and according to what rules. There's a big and vital difference between the unexplained and the inexplicable, and we should keep that in mind when discussing so-called psychic phenomena. Actually, I prefer the term 'wild talents,' which was coined by the science fiction writer Jack Vance." [16]

When asked why he thought parapsychological investigation is not well regarded in mainstream science, King responded, "Because they [the scientists] can't see it. They can't wear it. It's as simple as that. You're dealing with empirical results from something that can't be seen or weighed or felt or hefted or split in a cyclotron. You're talking about people that might have 20 hits out of 25 on those Rhine cards at Duke, and what scientists are reduced to saying is, 'Well, hey, he did it. But it was coincidence.' Even if the odds may be millions and millions to one."[17]

Whatever the truth regarding psychic phenomena, Stephen King has used some of these phenomena to good effect in several of his books. In *Carrie* the protagonist has the ability to make objects move by themselves and create spontaneous combustion. Throughout most of the book, Carrie is afraid of her special powers, but in the end she uses them in striking back at those who have made her life miserable.

In *The Shining* a young boy, Danny, has special powers also. Danny has the gift to see things that others cannot, a talent for precognition. An old man at the deserted resort hotel where Danny is staying with his parents calls Danny's gift "shining" and describes it to the child:

> "You got a knack," Halloran said, turning to him. "Me, I've always called it shining. That's what my grandmother called it,

too. She had it. We used to sit in the kitchen when I was a boy no older than you and have long talks without even openin [sic] our mouths." . . .

He said: "What you got, son, I call it shinin [sic] on, the Bible calls it having visions, and there's scientists that call it precognition. I've read up on it son. I've studied on it. They all mean seeing the future. Do you understand that?" . . .

"Well, that's how it is in this hotel. I don't know why, but it seems all the bad things that ever happened here, there's little pieces of those things still layin [sic] around like fingernail clippins [sic] or the boogers that somebody nasty just wiped under a chair. I don't know why it should just be here, there's bad goings-on in just about every hotel in the world, I guess, and I've worked in a lot of them and had no trouble. Only here. But, Danny, I don't think those things can hurt anybody."[18]

But the bad things in the hotel do end up hurting Danny's father, who becomes insane. In the climax Danny and his mother escape death, but old Hallorann is killed. Danny's father dies too, and the old hotel burns to the ground in a fiery end to the terrible things in the building.

Dead Zone is also a story of precognition. Here Johnny Smith suffers a coma as a young man and, when he finally awakens, finds he has the gift of seeing into the future. In the new life he must build for himself Johnny meets a presidential hopeful. Foreseeing the future, Johnny realizes that this man is an aspiring despotic dictator, and Johnny decides it is his duty, perhaps even his mission, to assassinate the candidate.

One of King's most popular psychic characters is probably Charlie McGee, a little girl central to the novel *Firestarter*. Her parents having taken part in government drug studies when they were college students, Charlie has been born with the ability of pyrokinesis. The government, in particular the agents in "The Shop," now want the results of their experiments, the child who can start fires. First they kill Charlie's mother. Charlie's father starts running with his daughter in an effort to save her. Eventually they are captured, but Charlie's wild talent helps her get away. In the end she turns to the power of the media, and all the readers of *Firestarter* hope that Charlie's story is told and that she is finally safe.

Stephen King and the Supernatural

As indicated, horror literature is often associated with the supernatural. Those who like to classify fiction according to genre sometimes think a piece of fiction must have a supernatural element to make it true horror. Although King is always called a horror writer, certainly a number of his works might also be classified as thrillers, psychological suspense, epics, fantasy, or science fiction. Yet all his stories contain an underlying current of terror and fright, those things which make horror what it is. This quality is hard to define precisely, because it is something each person feels on a personal and unique level.

If one accepts the argument that real horror literature should be about the supernatural, then only some of King's novels fall into that category: *'Salem's Lot, The Shining, Christine, Cycle of the Werewolf, Pet Sematary,* and *It.* Books about vampires (even when they live in Maine), haunted hotels, and slobbering werewolves qualify nicely, as does the tale of Christine, the rotten haunted car. Two, *Pet Sematary,* published in 1983, and *It,* published in 1986, are particularly interesting to examine for their supernatural themes, themes that show King at his dark-fantasy best.

Pet Sematary involves ghouls and the undead—beings resurrected from death, yet not truly living and somehow changed into evil, corruption, and decay. Although the basic premise is borrowed from the well-known short story by W. W. Jacobs, "The Monkey's Paw," *Pet Sematary* goes further. The situation described in the book was brought about not through hatred but through love—which makes it all the more terrifying. The father of a typical nuclear family, Louis Creed, first brings his daughter's dear cat, Churchill, back from death because she misses her pet so much. But the smell of death is on the cat, and Churchill is no longer the lovable furball he once was. Church should have stayed dead in the pet cemetery.

But Louis has not learned anything from this experience, and when his son, Gage, is killed by a truck in front of the house, Louis takes his son's body to the pet cemetery in order to have Gage restored to life. And Gage *is* restored, though not as the nice child he had been but, rather, as a foulmouthed, evil being. Gage too should have stayed dead. Louis knows he must take Gage back to the realm of the dead, but it is too late for Louis to return to any kind of life of normalcy, for he has meddled in awesome things that send him on a journey to madness.

Pet Sematary is one of King's best-crafted novels, nicely plotted and very controlled. It illustrates his skill as a storyteller and his delight in imparting a spine-tingling tale to breathless readers. Even though this book relies on traditional horror story devices, such as prophetic dreams of terrible things to come, *Pet Sematary* can be considered a modern classic of the genre.[19]

This book has a particularly painful history for King. He got the idea for the book when his own daughter's cat was run over and she reacted with hurt and rebellion. It is a book with other memories of bad times, and it is a book he does not talk about very often. Yet according to Douglas E. Winter, "Precisely because of King's closeness to its subject matter, *Pet Sematary* is one of the most vivid, powerful, and disturbing tales he has written. His hallmarks—effortless, colloquial prose, and an unerring instinct for the visceral—are in evidence throughout, but this novel succeeds because of King's ability to produce characters so familiar that they may well have lived next door for years" (*Art,* 132). Here again, King's depiction of wonderful characters is pinpointed as a reason for his success in writing. In this story the people are indeed believable and likable, and so we feel for them intensely, relating to their sorrows and anguish over death.

Whereas *Pet Sematary* ends on a typical horror story note of pessimism and the inevitable, *It* presents a different theme: the eternal struggle between good and evil, with good prevailing in the end. The plot of *It* seems deceptively simple for the novel's length, yet the book tells a story of great strength. It is an epic, rather on the order of King's epic, *The Stand*.

In many ways the protagonist of *It* is a town called Derry, Maine, based on King's boyhood hometown of Stratford, Connecticut. Living beneath the town is an evil monster, one often embodied as a clown, Pennywise. Pennywise likes to munch on children, who disappear with regularity on a 27-year cycle in order to feed his appetite. To make his food more palatable, Pennywise appears to his victims in advance so that they will be overcome by fear, apparently Pennywise's preferred seasoning. Pennywise can take on any form and chooses that which he knows will terrify each victim the most, be it a werewolf, a giant spider, or a clown. In actuality Pennywise is that universal evil known in all cultures—an ancient alien from another place or dimension—which aspect gives credence to his ability to take whatever form he selects.

King himself views *It* as an important work, since it pits two themes/characters he has used a number of times, monsters and children. The side of good in *It* is represented by several children who try to defeat the terrible Pennywise in their youth. They only wound him, however, and so 27 years later they return to Derry in their adulthood, prepared to battle the frightful evil to the end. This time they are not grade-school kids and they know how important it is for them to win, for if they lose, the evil may continue forever.

One of the central characters, Bev, serves as a mother figure for the rest as they remember what had happened to them as children and face new ordeals as adults. It is important that they have remembered, however, for in their remembering they touch on the innocence and magic of youth, qualities that in the end help them to defeat Pennywise in all his guises.

This belief in the power of childish innocence is described by Tony Magistrale: "King's romantic perception of childhood offers to light the way to moral excellence by helping man to distinguish between, and understand the nature of, good and evil. As Bill Denbrough comes fully to understand at the conclusion of *It*, the imaginative faith of childhood was given to man to guide him through life. It can help him envision the moral constitution of the world; it can explain the nature of the human animal and its natural imperfections; it can even lead him to the threshold of recreating his personality and identity."[20]

One of the most prolific commentators on King's work, Michael Collings, agrees with Magistrale about the importance of the protagonists' recapturing the essence of childhood in order to succeed in their struggle with the monster. In fact, Collings praises this book highly by saying, "Although it has its share of crudities and harsh language, violence, and stylistic infelicities (including repetitions that may simply be inevitable in a novel, the manuscript for which is, as King puts it, bigger than his own head), at the end, *It* transcends itself, to stand as the most powerful novel King has yet written" (Collings, 25).

Another analyst, Joseph Grixti, however, explains that "if this reading of King's account is correct, children's imaginations are more psychotic than psychic—and as we have seen, King believes that periodic psychotic flings are salutary. The trouble with adults, the argument suggests, is that they generally lose contact with the woe and wonder of incomprehensible irrationality."[21]

Summing Up

As an aspiring author, Stephen King schooled himself to write every day. With his enormous success, he now often mentions retiring from writing, but that doesn't seem to happen. In the waning days of summer 1990 King published another book, *Four Sides to Midnight,* a collection of four novellas. Perhaps a real storyteller can't stop telling stories. As a reviewer of this new work said,

> These four tales stand strongly on their own. They all demonstrate the qualities that have made King by far the world's most popular author: careful attention to background detail, generous layering of incident and anecdote, and marathon talent for maintaining a breathless pace. . . .

> A powerful storyteller knows the needs of his audience, un-
> derstands when to pause and when to pick up speed, when to
> shift the point of view and when not to.[22]

King says there are three levels of horror. The first and probably the finest is terror, in which the mind is horrified by what is
merely suggested by the author. An example might be Jacobs's
"The Monkey's Paw." The second level is fear, as illustrated by the
E. C. Comics of the 1950s. The third level is out-and-out revulsion, like that created by the torso-bursting scene in the movie
Alien. While using all three levels himself, King recognizes the
differences (*Macabre,* 34). And though literary critics may prefer
and praise the first level of terror and deplore the excesses of
revulsion, all three levels are legitimate forms of horror fiction.
As King himself has said, "On gore, I feel pretty much as Hitch
[Alfred Hitchcock] did: if you need to let it flow, man, let it *go*.
This is particularly effective if you do it well near the beginning
of a novel or film. . . . Violence for the sake of violence is of course
immoral and thus pornographic; to shy from a violent scene necessary to the story is equally immoral and equally pornographic"
(*Mystery Scene,* 4).

10. The Future of Horror Fiction

The popularity of certain types of fiction, including horror, seems to go through alternating periods of greater and lesser readership. For example, in the past decade mysteries have been very popular, westerns not. It is normal for publishers to respond to these cycles because publishing houses are in the business of making money, and it follows that the books with the greatest sales potential are those most likely to be published. It only makes sense for publishers to produce books that people want— a basic principle of the law of supply and demand.

Although horror fiction has been very popular with some readers for the past couple of decades, there are signs that enthusiasm for traditional horror tales may be waning. Fewer new titles are being published (although reprints are still common, particularly in paperback editions), and certain trends can be seen that may be considered clues to a dwindling enthusiasm for the genre.

Any genre has certain basic plots and devices. When these become overused and are not treated in a fresh, original way, the genre becomes boring. Horror readers like thrills and chills. If they find they are getting the same old thing over and over again, the scares don't come, and so why bother to read the books? If a product doesn't deliver what it promises, future sales are lost—a basic rule of marketing. If consumers are disappointed in a horror book, they may not purchase other books by the same author. Eventually those readers may desert the genre completely if a number of books do not meet their expectations.

Another clue to the saturation of a genre is the use of multiple devices in a single story. It may no longer be possible for an author to generate fright through a simple vampire, and so it may be necessary to include a werewolf and a mummy as well in the same story. Even Stephen King is guilty of this practice. As he remarked wryly in an interview for *Penthouse,* "I got everything in this book. I got Frankenstein, Jaws, the Creature from the Black Lagoon—fucking King Kong is in this book. I mean, it's like the monster rally. Everybody is there. I thought it would be a good one to go out with. Called *It.* I should call it *Shit.*"[1]

An editor in the field of horror has speculated:

> Things are tough in the publishing business right now. Industry figures show profits down across the board for the third year in a row. This means profit margins are tighter than ever, and publishers are naturally going to be extra careful about risk. So I'm afraid what I predict in the short term is that money will continue to be spent on known authors, because there are some guarantees built in, and even less than usual will go to unknown authors, where the risk is greatest. Think of horror in particular, there seem to be the 50,000 copy books and the million copy books and not much in between. Over the slightly longer term it will be interesting to see whether some more writers currently being in category numbers can go on to sell enough copies to put their names in that middle ground. Horror is going through a healthy retrenchment, and I believe it will emerge stronger than it is now.[2]

The next decade will probably see fewer traditional horror books. Those authors who have become mainstream writers, such as Stephen King, Dean Koontz, and Anne Rice, will continue to be published as long as their books sell well. Formula books, such as the seemingly endless stream of posthumous V. C. Andrews titles, will provide teens and others with the works of a favorite "author." Some of today's horror writers are breaking out of the mold and into other genres and mainstream fiction. There will probably be more crossover writing, resulting in books that cannot easily be classified as one genre or another. Publishers will be less likely to slap the "horror" label on any book with scary scenes.

A form of nonfiction that describes true crime in detail has drawn some readers away from supernatural horror and into the world of real-life horror. This type of "fiction" is apparently the hottest new genre of the year. Bookstores are creating specially marked sections for it. Interestingly enough, some of the readers of this "new" genre don't like more traditional horror stories. They prefer to read about the real thing, claiming to be interested in the psychological factors of twisted minds and perpetrators of bizarre crimes. For many readers, horror is better found in the true accounts of society today, rather than in the relatively harmless world of dark fantasy created by imaginative authors.

Horror literature has matured greatly with its recent popularity. It has become more respected by readers and even some critics. A few of these critics, unfortunately, try to inject a degree of literary depth probably unintended by the majority of horror writers. Other more thoughtful analysts have helped define the field. For example, Douglas E. Winter has discussed his criteria for standards of excellence in horror literature:

1. Originality, producing a feeling of horror in the reader
2. Characterization of people in the story who are human and likable
3. Reality based on the real world, not on a romanticized setting
4. Mystery that is not resolved
5. Bad taste that goes beyond conventionally accepted behavior
6. Suggestion, which is more effective than graphic detail
7. Subtext that creates a lasting impression
8. Subversion that is embodied by breaking rules
9. Monsters of today, such as Stephen King's "Trucks"
10. An endgame in which the reader is returned to the real world.[3]

Debating such questions is interesting from an intellectual point of view, though hardly necessary for the survival of the horror genre. Throughout this book a question has been raised (and not answered) as to whether or not supernatural elements need to be present in order to classify a book as horror fiction. Similarly, there has long been a category of fiction dealing with psychological horror that doesn't fall easily into any one of the presently acknowledged genres. It's not mystery, although certainly such books are thrillers. A number of horror writers have included such psychological stories in their repertoires. In the end, a book will probably be classified as horror if it horrifies the reader—particularly if that genre is selling well at the time.

It has been suggested by critics and publishers that horror literature does not thrive in times of war: real-life worries and concerns are too close, and people want escape by means of more comforting forms of fiction. It might, then, be cautiously concluded that horror literature does well in times of peace. With the threat of any immediate major confrontation between East and West removed with the end of the cold war, perhaps horror literature will enjoy a quick burst of renewed popularity in the years ahead.

This resurge of popularity probably will not happen, however, for often the vague cyclical laws that govern things such as popularity will produce a downswing. But the downswing will eventually bottom out—exactly when is uncertain.[4] Horror literature will again become as popular as it was in the 1980s—perhaps even more so. It will not totally disappear as a genre, but there will probably not be as many horror books published in the next decade, and they will not be as easy to find in stores and libraries as they have been. For those who are diehard horror fans, a word of advice: hang onto what you have and stock up, for there may well be a few lean years ahead.

But don't despair. Horror fiction will not die. It will return, rejuvenated by old and new writers and, most important, by a new generation of horror readers who appreciate a good scare now and then. Like that generic evil of many horror stories which can never be totally destroyed, the literature of horror may be dormant for a while but can't be eliminated altogether. The persistent and universal appeal of a good scary story will guarantee the ultimate survival of the horror genre.

Notes and References

1. The OK Factor in Horror

1. Judith Appelbaum, "Paperback Talk," *New York Times Book Review,* 30 October 1983, 39; hereafter cited in text.
2. Clifford Brooks and John Scoleri, "1988: A Novel Year," *Scream Factory,* Summer 1989, 10.
3. *Library Hotline,* 5 February 1990, 4.
4. Graham Masterton, "Horror of Horrors," *Writer,* August 1987, 15; hereafter cited in text.
5. Henry Kisor, "A Golden Nightmare of Odoriferous Terror from Stephen King," *Chicago Sun-Times,* 15 October 1989, 16.
6. On the upswing side, however, Katherine Ramsland reports that the International Association for the Fantastic in the Arts has formed a new section, the Lord Ruthven Assembly, for researches into the meaning of the vampire archetype (Katherine Ramsland, "Hunger for the Marvelous: The Vampire Craze in the Computer Age," *Psychology Today,* November 1989, 31).
7. Quoted in Mary Warner Marien, "Teen Fiction: Gore and Gruel Foster Shallow Self-Esteem," *Christian Science Monitor,* 2 December 1988, B2
8. Caryn James, "Yech! It's Jason, Dripping Soap," *New York Times,* 24 July 1988, H1
9. Quoted in Paul Freeman, "The Freddie Factor," *Chicago Tribune,* 6 November 1988, 31.
10. Elizabeth Massie, "Kids and Horror: Or, P. E. Can Wait, We've Got a Snot-sucking Vampire in Here!" *Horrorstruck,* September/October 1987, 13; hereafter cited in text.
11. D. W. Taylor, "The Perfect Horror Story," *Horrorstruck,* September/October 1987, 4, 42, and November/December 1987, 14–16; hereafter cited in text.

2. Horror and the Gothic Tradition: V. C. Andrews

1. Ann Radcliffe, *The Mysteries of Udolpho* (New York: Juniper Press, n.d.), 85.

2. Quoted in Douglas E. Winter, "V. C. Andrews," in *Faces of Fear* (New York: Berkley, 1985), 173; hereafter cited in text.

3. V. C. Andrews, *Dark Angel* (New York: Pocket Books, 1986), 444.

4. Quoted in Ida Kay Jordan, "From Book to Movie," *Currents,* 17 September 1980; hereafter cited in text.

5. Douglas Winter, "Writers of Today," in *The Penguin Encyclopedia of Horror and the Supernatural,* ed. Jack Sullivan (New York: Penguin, 1986), 471.

6. V. C. Andrews, *Flowers in the Attic* (New York: Pocket Books, 1979), 43; hereafter cited in text as *Flowers*.

7. Carolyn Banks, "Flowers in the Attic," *Washington Post,* 4 November 1979, 14.

8. V. C. Andrews, *Petals on the Wind* (New York: Pocket Books, 1980), 196; hereafter cited in text as *Petals*.

9. Bea Maxwell, "Petals in the Wind," *Los Angeles Times,* 5 October 1980, 15

10. V. C. Andrews, *If There Be Thorns* (New York: Pocket Books, 1981), 307; hereafter cited in text as *Thorns*

11. Dale Pollock, "If There Be Thorns," *Los Angeles Times,* 30 August 1981, 13

12. V. C. Andrews. *Seeds of Yesterday* (New York: Pocket Books, 1984), 371.

13. Kristiana Gregory, "Soft Cover," [*London*] *Times,* 29 April 1984, 10

14. "Seeds of Yesterday," *Publishers Weekly,* 27 January 1984, 72.

15. Patricia Miller, "Courage, Tragedy, Romance, Mystery: That's the Author—the Books Are Somewhat Different," [*London*] *Times,* 15 September 1982, 6

16. Robert F. Scott, "V. C. Andrews," in *Contemporary Authors,* New Revision series (Detroit: Gale Research, 1989), 21:24.

17. Eden Ross Lipson, "My Sweet Audrina," *New York Times Book Review,* 3 October 1982, 13

18. Florence King, *Southern Ladies and Gentlemen* (New York: Stein and Day, 1975), 167.

19. John Gilbert, "Tales from the Dark Side," *Fear,* June 1990, 7.

20. V. C. Andrews, *Dawn* (New York: Pocket Books, 1990), opposite verso of title page.

21. There is remarkable inconsistency throughout Andrews's books in the spellings of names, in addition to bad copyediting in general. Corrine is also spelled Corinne in the books, the version evidently adopted for the movie.

22. Harry McCracken, "Flowers in the Attic," *Cinefantastique,* May 1988, 44.

23. Quoted in Tony Germanotta, "Cancer Kills V. C. Andrews, Bestselling Local Novelist," *Virginia Pilot/Ledger Star,* 20 December 1986, A12

3. The Horror of Science: The Creations of Dean R. Koontz

1. James B. Twitchell, *Dreadful Pleasures: An Anatomy of Modern Horror* (New York: Oxford University Press, 1985), 175.

2. Quoted in Bill Munster, "Interview with Dean R. Koontz," in *Sudden Fear: The Horror and Dark Suspense Fiction of Dean R. Koontz,* ed. Bill Munster (Mercer Island, Wash.: Starmont, 1988), 29; hereafter cited in text.

3. "Dean R(ay) Koontz 1945–," *Contemporary Authors,* New Revision series, (Detroit: Gale Research, 1989), 19:267; hereafter cited in text as *Cont. Au.*

4. Mark Graham, "'80's Has Been Dean Koontz's Decade," *Blood Review,* January 1990, 51; hereafter cited in text.

5. Dean R. Koontz, "Interview with Dean R. Koontz," *Horror Show,* Summer 1987, 27.

6. David B. Silva, "Keeping Pace with the Master," in *Sudden Fear,* ed. Munster, 36.

7. Michael A. Morrison, "The Three Faces of Evil: The Monsters of *Whispers, Phantoms,* and *Darkfall,*" in *Sudden Fear,* ed. Munster, 116.

8. "Strangers," *Booklist,* 1 March 1986, 914.

9. Stan Brooks, "A Mutation of a Science Fiction Writer," in *Sudden Fear,* ed. Munster, 83.

10. "Watchers" *Kirkus Reviews,* 15 December 1986, 1817.

11. "Watchers," *Booklist,* 1 January 1987, 665.

12. Les Paul Robley, "Watchers," *Cinefantastique,* March 1990, 56.

13. Quoted in Sharon Pape, "Dean Koontz on Reading, Writing, and Breaking the 'Bestseller Barrier,'" in *How to Write Horror and Get It Published,* ed. Marc A. Cerasini (Brooklyn Heights, N.Y.: Romantic Times, 1989), 120.

14. Dean R. Koontz, *Twilight Eyes* (New York: Berkley, 1987), 183.

15. Mark Donovan, "Lightning," *People,* 30 April 1988, 30.

16. Michele Slung, "Lightning," *New York Times Book Review,* 3 April 1988, 14.

17. Marc A. Cerasini, "Dean Koontz and *Oddkins,*" *Rave Reviews,* Dec/Jan 1988–89, 14.

18. *New York Times Book Review,* 28 January 1990, 32.

19. Michael R. Collings, "The Bad Place," *Mystery Scene,* 82.

20. Quoted in Joe R. Lansdale, "Dean of Suspense," *Twilight Zone,* December 1986, 23.

4. The Eternal Struggle of Good and Evil: John Saul and Robert R. McCammon

1. Quoted in Laura Kramer, "John Saul: 'Remember, It's Only a Story,'" *Twilight Zone,* November 1981, 14; hereafter cited in text.

2. Andrea Chambers and Joni H. Blackman, "Careful Plotting for Success Lets Thriller Writer John Saul Enjoy All the 'Creature' Comforts," *People,* 26 June 1989, 80; hereafter cited in text.

3. James Kisner, "Interview: John Saul," *Mystery Scene,* 4; hereafter cited in text.

4. John Saul, *Suffer the Children* (New York: Bantam, 1977), 277; hereafter cited in text as *Suffer.*

5. As referred to in David M. Considine, *The Cinema of Adolescence* (Jefferson, N.C.: McFarland, 1985), 93.

6. Douglas Winter, "Writers of Today," in *The Penguin Encyclopedia of Horror and the Supernatural,* ed. Jack Sullivan (New York: Viking, 1986), 471.

7. Charles L. Grant, "The Gray Arena," in *Fear Itself: The Horror Fiction of Stephen King,* ed. Tim Underwood and Chuck Miller (San Francisco: Underwood-Miller, 1982), 147.

8. Stephen King, *Danse Macabre* (New York: Everest, 1981), 191.

9. Jackie Cassady, "Comes the Blind Fury," in *Library Journal Book Review 1980* (New York: Bowker, 1981), 667.

10. Quoted in Stanley Wiater, *Dark Dreamers: Conversations with the Masters of Horror* (New York: Avon, 1990) 180.

11. John R. Lansdale, "Interview: Robert R. McCammon," *Twilight Zone,* October 1986, 27; hereafter cited in text.

12. Charles de Lint, "Behind the Darkness—Profiles of the Writers of Horror Fiction: Robert R. McCammon—A Matter of Survival," *Horrorstruck,* May/June 1987, 30.

13. Robert R. McCammon, *The Night Boat* (New York: Avon, 1980), 133.

14. Robert R. McCammon, *They Thirst* (New York: Pocket Books, 1988), 563.

15. Matt Adler, "The Perils and Profits of Mixing Genres: The Work of Robert R. McCammon," in *How to Write Horror and Get It Published,* ed. Cerasini, 123; hereafter cited in text.

16. Douglas E. Winter, "The Art of Darkness," in *Shadowings: The Reader's Guide to Horror Fiction, 1981–1982,* ed. Douglas E. Winter (Mercer Island, Wash.: Starmont, 1983), 13.

17. Stanley Wiater, "Pro-files: A Sting in the Tale," *Fear,* November/ December 1988, 28.

18. Hunter Goatley, "The Robert R. McCammon Interview," *Lights Out! The Robert R. McCammon Newsletter,* July 1989, 9.

19. Robert R. McCammon, *Usher's Passing* (New York: Ballantine, 1985), 31.

20. Marc A. Cerasini, "From the Crypt," *Rave Reviews,* December/ January 1988–89, 80.

21. Sarah K. Martin, *School Library Journal,* October 1987, 146.

22. Eddy C. Bertin, "Swan Song," in *Horror: 100 Best Books,* ed. Stephen Jones and Kim Newman (New York: Carroll and Graf, 1988), 215.

23. Marc A. Cerasini, "Horror and the Occult," *Rave Reviews,* April/ May 1988, 75.

24. James Blair Lovell, "The Call of the Wild," *Book World,* 8 June 1989, 4.

25. Patrick Jones, *Voice of Youth Advocates,* August 1990, 168.

26. Charles de Lint, "Horror Review," *Mystery Scene,* 113.

27. Robert R. McCammon, "Innocence and Terror—The Heart of Horror," in *How to Write Tales of Horror, Fantasy and Science Fiction,* ed. J. N. Williamson (Cincinnati, Ohio: Writer's Digest Books, 1987), 69.

5. Monsters, Vampires, and Werewolves: The Sympathetic Beasts of Anne Rice and Chelsea Quinn Yarbro

1. James B. Twitchell, *Dreadful Pleasures: An Anatomy of Modern Horror* (New York: Oxford University Press, 1985); hereafter cited in text.

2. Quoted in W. Kenneth Holditch, "Interview with Anne Rice," *Lear's,* October 1989, 88–89; hereafter cited in text.

3. Quoted in Katherine Ramsland, "Anne Rice and the Children of the Night," *Magical Blend,* January 1990, 43; hereafter cited in text.

4. Katherine Ramsland, "Profile of Anne Rice," *Horror Show,* Spring 1990, 18.

5. Quoted in Mary Anne Cassata, "The Anne Rice Chronicles," *Inside Books,* July/August 1989, 31; hereafter cited in text.

6. Anne Rice, *Interview with the Vampire* (New York: Alfred Knopf, 1976), 102.

7. Edmund Fuller, "Sherlock Holmes Meets Dracula Man," *Wall Street Journal,* 17 June 1976, 10.

8. Pearl K. Bell, "Writers and Writing: A Gemeinschaft of Vampires," *New Leader,* 7 June 1976, 16.

9. Edith Milton, "Interview with the Vampire," *New Republic,* 8 May 1976, 29.

10. Anne Rice, *The Vampire Lestat* (New York: Alfred Knopf, 1985), 499, 501.

11. "Anne Rice, Author of *Queen of the Damned,*" *Bestsellers,* 18 August 1989, 72.

12. Anne Rice, *Queen of the Damned* (New York: Alfred Knopf, 1989), 573.

13. *Kirkus Reviews,* 1 September 1988, 1270.

14. Carl Hendricks, "The Queen of the Damned," *Rave Reviews,* October/November 1989, 75.

15. Eric Kraft, "Do Not Speak Ill of the Undead," *New York Times Book Review,* 27 November 1988, 13.

16. Anne Rice, *The Mummy* (New York, Alfred Knopf, 1989), dedication page; hereafter cited in text as *Mummy.*

17. Katherine Ramsland, "Anne Rice: Seeking Recognition as a Real Writer," *Blood Review,* January 1990, 34.

18. Frank J. Prial, "The Mummy," *New York Times Book Review,* 11 June 1989, 9.

19. Michael Rogers, "The Mummy," *Library Journal,* 1 April 1989, 114.

20. Quoted in Kitty Perdone, "Blood Sisters," *Midnight Graffiti,* Fall 1989, 48; hereafter cited in text.

21. Charles L. Grant, a friend of Chelsea Quinn Yarbro, refers to her as Quinn in his introduction to her collection of short stories, *Signs and Portents* (New York: Jove, 1987); hereafter cited in text as *Signs.*

22. Unless otherwise noted, biographical material on Chelsea Quinn Yarbro is taken from Thomas Wiloch, "Chelsea Quinn Yarbro," in *Contemporary Authors,* New Revision series, (Detroit: Gale Research, 1989), 25: 499–502; hereafter cited in text.

23. Stephen King, *Danse Macabre* (New York: Everest House, 1981), 75.

24. James Webb, "Comte de St-Germain," in *Man, Myth, and Magic: The Illustrated Encyclopedia of Mythology, Religion, and the Unknown* (New York: Marshall Cavendish, 1983), 9: 2460.

25. Gil Fitzgerald, "History as Horror: Chelsea Quinn Yarbro," in *Discovering Modern Horror Fiction,* ed. Darrell Schweitzer (Mercer Island, Wash.: Starmont, 1988), 2:133.

26. Chelsea Quinn Yarbro, *A Candle for D'Artagnan* (New York: TOR, 1989), 484.

27. Carol A. Senf, "Blood, Eroticism, and the Vampire in Twentieth-century Popular Literature," in *The Gothic World of Stephen King: Landscape of Nightmares,* ed. Gary Hoppenstand and Ray B. Browne (Bowling Green, Ohio: Bowling Green State University Popular Press, 1987), 23.

28. Brian J. Frost, *The Monster with a Thousand Faces: Guises of the Vampire in Myth and Literature* (Bowling Green, Ohio: Bowling Green State University Popular Press, 1989), 113, 116.

29. Carol A. Senf, *The Vampire in 19th Century English Literature* (Bowling Green, Ohio: Bowling Green State University Popular Press, 1988), 10.

30. Vincent Price and V. B. Price, *Monsters* (New York: Grosset and Dunlap, 1981), 92.

31. *Booklist,* August 1983, 1450.

32. *Publishers Weekly,* 1 April 1983, 58.

33. Audrey Eaglen, *Voice of Youth Advocates,* October 1983, 210.

34. Chelsea Quinn Yarbro, *Dead and Buried* (New York: Warner, 1980), 304.

6. Satanism, Cults, and Teens

1. Geraldo Rivera, "Geraldo: From Prison: Young Devil Worshippers," 29 November 1988 (New York: Journal Graphics, 1988), transcript 314.

2. Vickie L. Dawkins and Nina Downey Higgins, *Devil Child* (New York: St. Martin's Press, 1989), 272.

3. Robert J. Simandl, conference on "Satanism, Cults, and Law Enforcement," Northern Illinois University, DeKalb, Illinois, 7 February 1990.

4. Anton LaVey, *The Satanic Bible* (New York: Avon, 1969), and *The Satanic Rites* (New York: Avon, 1972).

5. Maury Terry, *The Ultimate Evil* (New York: Bantam, 1989). A skeptic's view of Terry's "proof" about the existence of "The Process" can

be found in Arthur Lyons's *Satan Wants You* (New York: Mysterious Press, 1988), 92.

6. "The Devil Is Alive and Hiding on Central Park West," *Time*, 23 June 1967, 102.

7. Douglas Fowler, *Ira Levin* (Mercer Island, Wash.: Starmont, 1988), 3.

8. Diane D. Vogel, "The All Time Horror Bestseller List," *Horror-struck*, July/August 1988, 11.

9. The word *cult*, as used in this context, refers to continued popularity of a film based on a following by people who appreciate the weird and the different.

10. Gerald W. Page, "Conjure Wife," in *Horror: 100 Best Books*, ed. Jones and Newman, 103.

11. Two quickly produced true-crime books have been written about this case: Gary Provost, *Across the Border: The True Story of the Satanic Cult Killings in Matamoros, Mexico* (New York: Pocket Books, 1989), and Jim Schutze, *Cauldron of Blood: The Matamoros Cult Killings* (New York: Avon, 1989).

12. *Kirkus Reviews*, 1 March 1982, 285.

13. Howard Witt, "A Fantasy Game and a Deadly Reality," *Chicago Tribune*, 27 January 1985, 3.

14. William Dear, *The Dungeon Master: The Disappearance of James Dallas Egbert III* (Boston: Houghton Mifflin, 1984).

7. True Crime and Imagination: Three Books by Robert Bloch

1. Robert Bloch, "Heritage of Horror," introduction to *The Dunwich Horror and Others*, by H. P. Lovecraft (Sauk City, Wis.: Arkham House, 1963), xxvi.

2. Quoted in Jean W. Ross, "Bloch, Robert (Albert), 1917–," in *Contemporary Authors*, New Revision series (Detroit: Gale Research, 1989), 5: 63; hereafter cited in text.

3. Randall D. Larson, *Robert Bloch*, Starmont Reader's Guide 37 (Mercer Island, Wash.: Starmont, 1986), 10; hereafter cited in text.

4. Douglas E. Winter, in *Faces of Fear*, 13; hereafter cited in text.

5. Richard Christian Matheson, "They Laughed When I Howled at the Moon," in *How to Write Tales of Horror, Fantasy, and Science Fiction*, ed. Williamson, 120.

6. Harold Schechter, *Deviant: The Shocking True Story of the Original "Psycho"* (New York: Pocket Books, 1989).

7. Stephen King, *Danse Macabre* (New York: Everest, 1981), 84.

8. Quoted in Don C. Thompson, "Writer's Bloch: Weekend with a Legend," *Blood Review,* January 1990, 6.

9. Robert Bloch, *Psycho* (New York: Simon and Schuster, 1959), 51; hereafter cited in text as *Psycho.*

10. David Punter, "Robert Bloch's *Psycho*: Some Pathological Contexts," in *American Horror Fiction,* ed. Brian Docherty (Houndmills, Basingstoke, Hampshire, England: Macmillan, 1990), 94.

11. Hugh B. Cave, "Psycho," in *Horror: 100 Best Books,* ed. Jones and Newman, 126.

12. David J. Hogan, *Dark Romance: Sexuality in the Horror Film* (Jefferson, N.C.: McFarland, 1986), 235.

13. Quoted in Stanley Wiater, "Bloch of Prose," *Fear,* January 1990, 10.

14. Quoted in Randall D. Larson, ed., *The Robert Bloch Companion: Collected Interviews—1969–1989* (Mercer Island, Wash.: Starmont, 1989), 121.

15. Robert Bloch, "How to Write Horribly for Fun and Profit," in *How to Write Tales of Horror, Fantasy, and Science Fiction,* ed. Williamson, 9.

16. June Sawyers, "Dark Doings by a South Side Bluebeard." *Chicago Tribune Magazine,* 25 October 1987, 9.

17. Robert Bloch, "Dr. Holmes's Murder Castle," in *Tales of the Uncanny,* selected by the editors of *Reader's Digest* (Pleasantville, N.Y.: Reader's Digest, 1983), 9.

18. Robert Bloch, "Monsters in Our Midst," in *Kingdom of Fear: The World of Stephen King,* ed. Tim Underwood and Chuck Miller (San Francisco: Underwood-Miller, 1986), 26.

19. Robert Bloch, foreword to *Ripper!,* ed. Gardner Dozois and Susan Casper (New York: TOR, 1988), xv.

20. Robert Bloch, "Yours Truly, Jack the Ripper," in *Ripper!,* ed. Dozois and Casper, 119.

21. Randall D. Larson, "Yours Truly, Robert Bloch," in *Discovering Modern Horror Fiction,* ed. Schweitzer, 2:67.

22. Dozois and Casper, eds., *Ripper!,* 100. Additional comments about Bloch's skill as a short story writer can be found in, among other places, Edgar F. Tatro's essay "Prose and Conversation: Horror Stories, A Teacher's Perspective" (*New Blood Magazine,* Fall 1988, 32).

23. A thorough examination of existing theories to date, including Bloch's, can be found in Donald Rumbelow, *Jack the Ripper: The Complete Casebook* (New York: Berkley, 1990).

24. Quoted in Jack Hitt, ed., "In Pursuit of Pure Horror," *Harper's,* October 1989, 50.

25. Robert Bloch, *The Night of the Ripper* (New York: Doubleday, 1984), 285.

8. A Pause for Splatterpunk

1. Stefan Dziemianowicz, "Splatterpunk: Invasion of the Body Slashers," in *How to Write Horror and Get It Published*, ed. Cerasini, 80; hereafter cited in text.
2. Quoted in James Kisner, "Interview with Ray Garton," *Mystery Scene*, January 1990, 84.
3. Quoted in Jessie Horsting, "The Splat Pack," *Midnight Graffiti*, June 1988, 31; hereafter cited in text.
4. John Russo, "'Reel' vs. Real Violence," *Newsweek*, 19 February 1990, 10.
5. Quoted in Clifford Brooks, "An Interview with Richard Christian Matheson," *Scream Factory*, Summer 1989, 34.
6. Quoted in Sarah Wood, "Ray Garton: Is There Such a Thing as Too Much?" *Midnight Graffiti*, Fall 1988, 28.
7. "An Interview with Ray Garton," *Gauntlet*, premier issue (1990), 28; hereafter cited in text as *Gauntlet*.
8. Ray Garton, *Crucifax* (New York: Pocket Books, 1988), 171.
9. John Skipp and Craig Spector, *The Light at the End* (New York: Bantam, 1987), 372.
10. Quoted in Wiater, *Dark Dreamers*, 186.
11. "The Scream: A Tale of Two Splatterpunks." *Fear*, July–August 1988, 24.
12. "Works in Progress—David J. Schow," *Fear*, March 1990, 31.
13. Charles de Lint, "Behind the Darkness," *Horrorstruck*, May/June 1988, 25; hereafter cited in text.

9. The King of Dark Fantasy: Stephen King and Teens

1. "Interview with Stephen King," *Mystery Scene*, 4; hereafter cited in text as *Mystery Scene*.
2. Stephen King, *Danse Macabre* (New York: Everest, 1981), 25; hereafter cited in text as *Macabre*.
3. Quoted in Douglas Winter, "Stephen King," in *Faces of Fear*, 241.
4. Douglas Winter, *Stephen King: The Art of Darkness*, expanded

and updated ed. (New York: New American Library, 1986), 27; hereafter cited in text as *Art.*

5. Douglas E. Winter, "Talking Terror," *Twilight Zone,* February 1986, 16; hereafter cited in text as *TZ.*

6. Robert R. Harris, "Brand-Name Horror," *New York Times Book Review,* 27 November 1983, 43.

7. *The Gothic World of Stephen King: Landscape of Nightmares,* ed. Gary Hoppenstand and Ray B. Browne (Bowling Green, Ohio: Bowling Green State University Popular Press, 1987), 7.

8. Thomas F. Monteleone, "King's Characters: The Main(e) Heat," in *Kingdom of Fear,* ed. Underwood and Miller, 246.

9. Chelsea Quinn Yarbro, "Cinderella's Revenge—Twists on Fairy Tale and Mythic Themes in the Work of Stephen King," in *Fear Itself,* ed. Underwood and Miller, 46.

10. Tom Newhouse, "A Blind Date with Disaster: Adolescent Revolt in the Novels of Stephen King," in *The Gothic World of Stephen King,* ed. Hoppenstand and Browne, 52.

11. Tim Underwood, "The Skull beneath the Skin," in *Kingdom of Fear,* ed. Underwood and Miller, 256.

12. Richard Bleiler, "Stephen King," in *Supernatural Fiction Writers,* ed. Richard Bleiler (New York: Scribner's, 1985), 2: 1038.

13. Linda C. Badley, "Love and Death in the American Car: Stephen King's Auto-Erotic Horror," in *The Gothic World of Stephen King,* ed. Hoppenstand and Browne, 91.

14. William F. Nolan, "The Good Fabric: Of Night Shifts and Skeleton Crews," in *Kingdom of Fear,* ed. Underwood and Miller, 104.

15. Michael R. Collings, *The Stephen King Phenomenon* (Mercer Island, Wash.: Starmont, 1987), 24; hereafter cited in text.

16. Quoted in Eric Norden, "The *Playboy* Interview," in *The Stephen King Companion,* ed. George Beahm (Kansas City: Andrews and McMeel, 1989), 21.

17. Quoted in "With Martha Thomases and John Robert Tebbel (*High Times*)," in *Bare Bones: Conversations on Terror with Stephen King,* ed. Tim Underwood and Chuck Miller (New York: Warner, 1989), 198.

18. Stephen King, *The Shining* (New York: Doubleday, 1977), 79, 86.

19. This is not the opinion of Tim Underwood in his essay "The Skull beneath the Skin" (see note 11), in which he describes the book as "not the best written or constructed" (261). An essay on various criticisms of King's work can be found in Collings, *The Stephen King Phenomenon,* 60.

20. Tony Magistrale, *Landscape of Fear: Stephen King's American Gothic* (Bowling Green, Ohio: Bowling Green State University Popular Press, 1988), 121.

21. Joseph Grixti, *Terror of Uncertainty: The Cultural Contexts of Horror Fiction* (London: Routledge, 1989), 62.

22. Robert Chatain, "King of the Creeps," *Chicago Tribune Books,* 26 August 1990, 3.

10. The Future of Horror Fiction

1. Quoted in Bob Spitz, "Dancing in the Dark," in *Bare Bones,* ed. Underwood and Miller, 191.

2. "Susan Allison of the Berkley Publishing Group," *Mystery Scene,* 102.

3. Douglas E. Winter, "Darkness Absolute: The Standards of Excellence in Horror Fiction," in *How to Write Tales of Horror, Fantasy, and Science Fiction,* ed. Williamson, 156.

4. Thirty-five years has been suggested as a popularity cycle for literature (Thomas J. Roberts, *An Aesthetics of Junk Fiction* [Athens: University of Georgia Press, 1990], 201).

Selected Bibliography and Filmography

V. C. Andrews

Primary Sources

Novels

Dark Angel. New York: Pocket Books, 1986.
Dawn. New York: Pocket Books, 1990 (authorship questionable).
Fallen Hearts. New York: Pocket Books, 1988.
Flowers in the Attic. New York: Pocket Books, 1979.
Garden of Shadows. New York: Pocket Books, 1987.
Gates of Paradise. New York: Pocket Books, 1989. (authorship questionable)
Heaven. New York: Pocket Books, 1985.
If There Be Thorns. New York: Pocket Books, 1981.
My Sweet Audrina. New York: Pocket Books Hardcover, 1982.
Petals on the Wind. New York: Pocket Books, 1980.
Seeds of Yesterday. New York: Pocket Books, 1984.
Web of Dreams. New York: Pocket Books, 1990. (authorship questionable)

Secondary Sources

Langdon, Dolly. "Have You Read a Best-Selling Gothic Lately? Chances Are It Was by a Recluse Named V.C. Andrews." *People,* 6 October 1980, 51.
Scott, Robert F. "Andrews, V(irginia) C(leo) ?–1986." *Contemporary Authors* New Revision, vol. 21. Detroit: Gale Research, 1989, 23.
Winter, Douglas E. "V.C. Andrews." In his *Faces of Fear.* New York: Berkley, 1985, 163.

183

Filmography

Flowers in the Attic. A New World Pictures and Fries Entertainment presentation of a Charles Fries production. Director: Jeffrey Bloom. Released: November 1987. 95 min. Color. Screenplay by Jeffrey Bloom. Stars: Louise Fletcher, Victoria Tennant, Kristy Swanson, Jeb Stuart Adams, Ben Ganger, and Lindsay Parker.

Robert Bloch

Primary Sources

Novels and Collected works with Predominantly Horror/ Suspense Themes.

American Gothic. New York: Simon and Schuster, 1974. (An ALA Best Books for Young Adults, 1975).

Complete Stories of Robert Bloch. New York: Carol Publishing Group, 1987–.

Fear and Trembling. New York: TOR, 1989.

Firebug. New York: Regency, 1961.

The Kidnapper. New York: Lion, 1954.

Lori. New York: TOR, 1989.

The Night of the Ripper. New York: Doubleday, 1984.

Night-World. New York: Simon and Schuster, 1972.

Psycho. New York: Simon and Schuster, 1959.

Psycho House. New York: TOR, 1980.

Psycho II. New York: Warner, 1982.

Twilight Zone: The Movie. New York: Warner, 1983.

Screenplays

Asylum. Based on Bloch's stories "Frozen Fear," "The Weird Tailor," "Lucy Comes to Stay," and "Mannikins of Horror."

The House that Dripped Blood. Based on Bloch's stories "Method for Murder," "The Living End," "Sweets to the Sweet," and "The Cloak."

Torture Garden based on "Enoch," "Terror over Hollywood," "Mr. Steinway," and "The Man Who Collected Poe."

Secondary Sources

Randall D. Larson. *Robert Bloch*. Mercer Island, Wash.: Starmont, 1986.
————, ed. *The Robert Bloch Companion: Collected Interviews—1969–1989*. Mercer Island, Wash.: Starmont, 1989.

Filmography

Asylum (also entitled *"House of Crazies"*). Amicus/Harbour Productions. Director: Roy Ward Baker. Released: 1972. 88 min. Color. Screenplay by Robert Bloch. Stars: Patrick Magee, Robert Powell, Geoffrey Bayldon, Barbara Parkins, Sylvia Syms, Richard Todd, Peter Cushing, Carry Morse, Ana Firbank, Britt Ekland, Charlotte Rampling, James Villiers, Megs Jenkins, and Herbert Lom.
The House That Dripped Blood. Amicus. Director: Peter Duffel. Released: 1971. 102 min. Color. Screenplay by Robert Bloch. Stars: Denholm Elliott, Joanna Lumley, Tom Adams, Robert Lang, Peter Cushing, Joss Ackland, Wolfe Morris, Christopher Lee, Nyree Dawn Porter, Chloe Franks, Jon Pertwee, Ingrid Pitt, and John Bennett.
Psycho. Paramount. Director: Alfred Hitchcock. Released: 1960. 109 min. Black/white. Screenplay by Joseph Stefano. Stars: Anthony Perkins, Janet Leigh, Vera Miles, John Gavin, Martin Balsam, and John McIntyre.
The Skull. Amicus. Director: Freddie Francis. Released: 1965. 90 min. Black/white. Screenplay by Milton Subotsky. Stars: Peter Cushing, Christopher Lee, Jill Bennett, Patrick Wymark, Michael Gough, Nigel Green, George Coulouris, Patrick Magee, and Peter Woodthorpe.

Stephen King

Primary Sources

Only the first editions are included in this list.

Carrie. New York: Doubleday, 1974. (An ALA Best Book for Young Adults, 1974).

Christine. New York: Viking, 1983.

Creepshow. New York: New American Library, 1982.

Cujo. New York: Viking, 1981.

Cycle of the Werewolf. New York: New American Library, 1983.

Danse Macabre. New York: Everest House, 1981.

The Dark Half. New York: Viking, 1989.

The Dark Tower: The Gunslinger. New York: New American Library, 1982.

The Dead Zone, New York: Viking, 1979.

Different Seasons. New York: Viking, 1982.

The Drawing of the Three. New York: New American Library, 1989.

The Eyes of the Dragon. New York: Viking, 1984.

Firestarter. New York: Viking, 1980. (An ALA Best Book for Young Adults, 1980).

Four Past Midnight. New York: Viking, 1990.

It. New York: Viking, 1986.

The Long Walk (under the pseudonym Richard Bachman). New York: Signet, 1979. (An ALA Best Book for Young Adults, 1978).

Misery. New York: Viking, 1987.

My Pretty Pony. New York: Knopf, 1989.

Night Shift. New York: Doubleday, 1978. (An ALA Best Book for Young Adults, 1978).

Pet Sematary. New York: Doubleday, 1983.

Rage (under the pseudonym Richard Bachman). New York: Signet, 1977.

Roadwork (under the pseudonym Richard Bachman). New York: Signet, 1981.

The Running Man (under the pseudonym Richard Bachman). New York: Signet, 1982.

'Salem's Lot. New York: Doubleday, 1975.

The Shining. New York: Doubleday, 1977.

Skeleton Crew. New York: Putnam, 1985.

The Stand. New York: Doubleday, 1978; expanded edition. New York: Doubleday, 1990.

The Talisman (with Peter Straub). New York: Viking/Putnam, 1984.

Thinner (under the pseudonym Richard Bachman). New York: New American Library, 1984.

The Tommyknockers. New York: Putnam, 1987.

Secondary Sources

Beahm, George, ed. *The Stephen King Companion.* Kansas City, Mo.: Andrews and McMeel, 1989.

Blue, Tyson. *The Unseen King.* Mercer Island, Wash.: Starmont, 1990.

Collings, Michael R. *The Annotated Guide to Stephen King: A Primary and Secondary Bibliography of the Works of America's Premier Horror Writer.* Starmont Reference Guide 8. Mercer Island, Wash.: Starmont, 1986.

———. *The Films of Stephen King.* Starmont Studies in Literary Criticism 12. Mercer Island, Wash.: Starmont, 1986.

———. *The Many Facets of Stephen King.* Starmont Studies in Literary Critism 11. Mercer Island, Wash.: Starmont, 1986.

———. *Stephen King as Richard Bachman.* Starmont Studies in Literary Criticism 10. Mercer Island, Wash.: Starmont, 1985.

———. *The Stephen King Phenomenon.* Starmont Studies in Literary Criticism 14. Mercer Island, Wash.: Starmont, 1987.

———, and David Engebretson. *The Shorter Works of Stephen King.* Starmont Studies in Literary Criticism 9. Mercer Island, Wash.: Starmont, 1985.

Conner, Jeff. *Stephen King Goes to Hollywood.* New York: New American Library, 1987.

Herron, Don, ed. *Reign of Fear.* San Francisco, Calif.: Underwood-Miller, 1988.

Hoppenstand, Gary and Ray B. Browne, eds. *The Gothic World of Stephen King: Landscape of Nightmares.* Bowling Green, Ohio: Bowling Green State University Popular Press, 1987.

Horsting, Jessie. *Stephen King at the Movies.* New York: Starlog/Signet, 1986.

Magistrale, Tony. *Landscape of Fear: Stephen King's American Gothic.* Bowling Green, Ohio: Bowling Green State University Popular Press, 1988.

Reino, Joseph. *Stephen King: The First Decade, "Carrie" to "Pet Sematary."* New York: Twayne, 1988.

Schweitzer, Darrell, ed. *Discovering Stephen King.* Starmont Studies in Literary Criticism 8. Mercer Island, Wash: Starmont, 1985.

Underwood, Tim, and Chuck Miller, eds. *Bare Bones.* San Francisco, Calif.: Underwood-Miller, 1988.

———. *Fear Itself: The Horror Fiction of Stephen King.* San Francisco, Calif.: Underwood-Miller, 1982.

———. *Feast of Fear: Conversations with Stephen King.* San Francisco, Calif.: Underwood-Miller, 1989.

———. *Kingdom of Fear.* San Francisco, Calif.: Underwood-Miller, 1986.

Winter, Douglas. *Stephen King.* Starmont Reader's Guide 16. Mercer Island, Wash.: Starmont, 1982.

———. *Stephen King: The Art of Darkness.* New York: New American Library, 1984.

Zagorski, Edward J. *Teacher's Manual: Novels of Stephen King.* New York: New American Library, 1981.

Filmography

Carrie. United Artists. Director: Brian De Palma. Released: November 1976. 97 min. Color. Screenplay by Lawrence D. Cohen. Stars: Sissy Spacek, Piper Laurie, Amy Irving, William Katt, Nancy Allen, John Travolta, Betty Buckley, P. J. Soles, Priscilla Pointer, and Michael Talbot.

Cat's Eye. MGM/United Artists. Director: Lewis Teague. Released: August 1984. 94 min. Color. Screenplay by Stephen King. Stars: Drew Barrymore, James Woods, Alan King, Kenneth McMillan, Robert Hays, Candy Clark, James Naughton, and Tony Munafo.

Children of the Corn. New World/Angles/Inverness/Hal Roach/Cinema Group. Director: Fritz Kiersch. Released: June 1984. 93 min. Color. Screenplay by George Goldsmith. Stars: Peter Horton, Linda Hamilton, R. G. Armstrong, John Franklin, Courtney Gains, Robby Kiger, Annemarie McEvoy, Julie Maddalena, and Jonas Marlowe.

Christine. Columbia. Director: John Carpenter. Released: December 1983. 110 min. Color. Screenplay by Bill Phillips. Stars: Keith Gordon, John Stockwell, Alexandra Paul, Robert Prosky, Harry Dean Stanton, Christine Belford, Roberts Blossom, and William Ostrander.

Creepshow. Warner Brothers/UFD/Laurel. Director: George Romero. Released: October 1982. 120 min. Color. Screenplay by Stephen King. Stars: E. G. Marshall, Hal Holbrook, Adrienne Barbeau, Fritz Weaver, Leslie Nielsen, Carrie Nye, Viveca Lindfors, Ed Harris, Ted Danson, and Stephen King.

Creepshow 2. New World. Director: Michael Gormick. Released: 1987. 89 min. Color. Screenplay by George Romero. Stars: Lois Chiles, George Kennedy, Dorothy Lamour, Tom Savini, Domenick John, Frank S. Salsedo, Holt McCallany, David Holbrook, Page Hannah, and Stephen King.

Cujo. Warner Brothers/Taft. Director: Lewis Teague. Released: June 1983. 120 min. Color. Screenplay by Don Carlos Dunaway and Lauren Currier. Stars: Dee Wallace, Daniel Hugh-Kelly, Christopher Stone, Ed Lauter, Kaiulani Lee, Billy Jacobi, and Danny Pintauro.

The Dead Zone. Paramount. Director: David Cronenberg. Released: October 1983. 103 min. Color. Screenplay by Jeffrey Boam. Stars: Christopher Walken, Brooke Adams, Martin Sheen, Tom Skerritt, Herbert Lom, Colleen Dewhurst, Nicholas Campbell, Anthony Zerbe, Sean Sullivan, and Jackie Burroughs.

Firestarter. Universal/Dino De Laurentiis. Director: Mark L. Lester. Released: October 1984. 115 min. Color. Screenplay by Stanley Mann. Stars: David Keith, Drew Barrymore, Martin Sheen, George C. Scott, Art Carney, Louise Fletcher, Freddie Jones, Heather Locklear, and Moses Gunn.

Maximum Overdrive. De Laurentiis. Director: Stephen King. Released: August 1986. 95 min. Color. Screenplay by Stephen King. Stars: Emilio Estevez, Pat Hingle, Laura Harrington, Yeardley Smith, John Short, Ellen McElduff, J. C. Quinn, Christopher Murney, and Holter Graham.

Pet Sematary. Paramount. Director: Mary Lambert. Released: April 1989. 102 min. Color. Screenplay by Stephen King. Stars: Dale Midkiff, Fred Gwynne, Denise Crosby, Brad Greenquist, Miko Hughes, and Stephen King.

"'Salem's Lot." Warner Brothers. Director: Tobe Hooper. Released: November 1979, as a television miniseries. 200 min. Color. Screenplay by Paul Monash. Cast: David Soul, James Mason, Lance Kerwin, Bonnie Bedelia, Lew Ayres, Reggie Nalder, Julie Cobb, Geoffrey Lewis, Fred Willard, Kenneth McMillan, and Elisha Cook.

The Shining. Warner Brothers/Producer Circle Group. Director: Stanley Kubrick. Released: June 1980. 143 min. Color. Screenplay by Stanley Kubrick and Diane Johnson. Stars: Jack Nicholson, Shelley Duvall, Danny Lloyd, Scatman Crothers, Barry Nelson, Philip Stone, and Joe Turkel.

Silver Bullet. Paramount Picture/North Carolina/De Laurentiis. Director: Daniel Attias. Released: October 1985. 95 min. Color. Screenplay by Stephen King. Stars: Gary Busey, Everett McGill, Corey Haim, Megan Fellows, Robin Groves, Leon Russom, and Terry O'Quinn.

Stand by Me. Columbia Picture/Act III. Director: Rob Reiner. Released: September 1986. 110 min. Color. Screenplay by Raynold Gideon and Bruce A. Evans. Stars: Will Wheaton, River Phoenix, Corey Feldman, Jerry O'Connell, Richard Dreyfuss, Kiefer Sutherland, Bradley Gregg, and Casey Siemaszko. Based on "The Body," the "autumn" section of *Different Seasons.*

Dean R. Koontz

Primary Sources

Suspense and Horror Fiction

The Bad Place. New York: Putnam, 1990.

Chase (under the pseudonym K. R. Dwyer). New York: Random House, 1972.

Darkfall. New York: Berkley, 1984.

Demon Seed. New York: Bantam, 1973.

The Door to December (under the pseudonym Richard Paige). New York: New American Library, 1985.

The Eyes of Darkness (under the pseudonym Leigh Nichols). New York: Pocket Books, 1981.

The Funhouse (under the pseudonym Owen West). New York: Jove, 1980.

The House of Thunder (under the pseudonym Leigh Nichols). New York: Pocket Books, 1982.

The Key to Midnight (under the pseudonym Leigh Nichols). New York: Pocket Books, 1979.

Lightning. New York: Putnam, 1988.

The Mask (under the pseudonym Owen West). New York: Jove, 1981.

Midnight. New York: Putnam, 1989.

Night Chills. New York: Atheneum, 1976.

Nightmare Journey. New York: Putnam, 1975.

Phantoms. New York: Putnam, 1983.

Shadowfires (under the pseudonym Leigh Nichols). New York: Pocket Books, 1987.

Shattered (under the pseudonym K. R. Dwyer). New York: Random House, 1973.

Strangers. New York: Putnam, 1986.

Twilight (under the pseudonym Leigh Nichols). New York: Pocket Books, 1984.

Twilight Eyes. New York: Berkley, 1987. (First published by Land of Enchantment, 1985).

The Vision. New York: Putnam, 1977.

Watchers. New York: Putnam, 1987. (An ALA Best Book for Young Adults, 1987).

Whispers. New York: Putnam, 1980.

Nonfiction

How to Write Best-selling Fiction. Cincinnati, Ohio: Writer's Digest Books, 1981.

Writing Popular Fiction. Cincinnati, Ohio: Writer's Digest Books, 1973.

Secondary Source

Sudden Fear: The Horror and Dark Suspense Fiction of Dean R. Koontz.
Edited by Bill Munster. Mercer Island, Wash.: Starmont, 1988.

Filmography

Demon Seed. MGM, a Herb Jaffe Production. Director: Donald Cammel.
Released: 1977. 94 min. Color. Screenplay by Robert Jaffe and Roger
O. Hirson. Stars: Julie Christie and Fritz Weaver.
The Watchers. Watchers Productions Ltd. Director: Jon Hess. Released:
November 1988. 92 min. Color. Screenplay by Bill Freed and Dam-
ian Lee. Stars: Corey Haim, Barbara Williams, Michael Ironside,
and Lala.

Robert R. McCammon

Primary Sources

Baal. New York: Avon, 1978.
Bethany's Sin. New York: Avon, 1980.
Blue World. London: Grafton, 1989. New York: Pocket Books, 1990.
Mine. New York: Pocket Books, 1990.
Mystery Walk. New York: Holt, Rinehart and Winston, 1983. New York:
Ballantine, 1984.
The Night Boat. New York: Avon, 1980.
Stinger. New York: Pocket Books, 1988.
Swan Song. New York: Pocket Books, 1987.
They Thirst. New York: Pocket Books, 1981.
Usher's Passing. New York: Holt, Rinehart and Winston, 1984. New York:
Ballantine, 1985.
The Wolf's Hour. New York: Pocket Books, 1987.

Secondary Sources

Adler, Matt. "The Perils and Profits of Mixing Genres: The Work of Robert R. McCammon." In *How to Write Horror and Get It Published,*
edited by Marc A. Cerasini. Brooklyn Heights, N.Y.: Romantic
Times, 1989, 122.

de Lint, Charles. "Behind the Darkness—Profiles of the Writers of Horror Fiction: Robert R. McCammon—A Matter of Survival." *Horror-struck,* May/June 1987, 28, 38.

Lansdale, Joe R. "Interview: Robert R. McCammon." *Twilight Zone,* October 1986, 24.

Lights Out! The Robert R. McCammon Newsletter. Orem, Utah: Hunter Goatley, 1989–.

Wiater, Stanley. "Pro-file: A Sting in the Tale." *Fear,* November–December 1988, 26.

Anne Rice

Primary Sources

A Cry to Heaven. New York: Alfred Knopf, 1982. New York: Pinnacle, 1983.

The Feast of All Saints. New York: Simon and Schuster, 1979. New York: Fawcett, 1981.

Interview with the Vampire. New York: Alfred Knopf, 1976. New York: Ballantine, 1977.

The Mummy: Or Ramses the Damned. New York: Alfred Knopf, 1989.

Queen of the Damned. New York: Alfred Knopf, 1989. New York: Ballantine, 1989.

The Vampire Lestat. New York: Alfred Knopf, 1985. New York: Ballantine, 1986.

The Witching Hour. New York: Alfred Knopf, 1990.

Secondary Sources

Gates, David. "Queen of the Spellbinders." *Newsweek,* 5 November 1990, 76.

Holditch, W. Kenneth. "Interview with Anne Rice." *Lear's,* October 1989, 88.

Perdone, Kitty. "Blood Sisters." *Midnight Graffiti,* Fall 1989, 48.

Ramsland, Katherine. "Anne Rice and the Children of the Night." *Magical Blend,* January 1990, 43.

———. "Anne Rice: Seeking Recognition as Real Writer." *The Blood Review,* January 1990, 34.

———. "Profile of Anne Rice." *The Horror Show,* Spring 1990, 18.

Satanism, Cults, and Teens

Blatty, William Peter. *The Exorcist.* New York: Harper and Row, 1971.

Condé, Nicholas. *The Religion* (later released as *The Believers*). New York: New American Library, 1982.

Coyne, John. *Hobgoblin.* New York: G. P. Putnam's, 1981.

Dear, William. *The Dungeon Master: The Disappearance of James Dallas Egbert III.* Boston: Houghton Mifflin, 1985. (*School Library Journal* Best Young Adult Books List, 1985).

Goudge, Elizabeth. *The White Witch.* New York: Coward-McCann, 1958.

Hardy, Robin, and Shaffer, Anthony. *The Wicker Man.* New York: Crown, 1977.

Jaffe, Rona. *Mazes and Monsters.* New York: Delacorte, 1981. (An ALA Best Books for Young Adults, 1981).

Kurtz, Katherine. *Lammas Night.* New York: Crown, 1983.

Levin, Ira. *Rosemary's Baby.* New York: Random House, 1967.

Leiber, Fritz. *Conjure Wife.* New York: Twayne, 1953.

Waugh, Charles G., and Martin H. Greenberg, eds. *Cults! An Anthology of Secret Societies, Sects and the Supernatural.* New York: Beaufort, 1983.

Wheatley, Dennis. *The Devil Rides Out.* London: Hutchinson, 1935.

Filmography

The Believers. Orion Pictures. Director: John Schlesinger. Released: 1987. 114 min. Color. Screenplay by Mark Frost. Stars: Martin Sheen, Helen Shaver, Harley Cross, Robert Loggia, Elizabeth Wilson, Lee Richardson, Harris Yulin, Richard Masur, Carla Pinza, and Jimmy Smits.

Children of the Corn. New World. Director: Fritz Kiersch. Released: 1984. 92 min. Color. Screenplay by George Goldsmith. Stars: Peter Horton, Linda Hamilton, R. G. Armstrong, John Franklin, and Courtney Gains.

The *Conjure Wife* films (in chronological order):

Weird Woman. Universal. Director: Reginald LeBorg. Released: 1944. 63 min. Black/white. Screenplay by Brenda Weisberg. Stars: Lon Chaney, Jr.; Anne Gwynne; Evelyn Ankers; Ralph Morgan; Lois Collier; and Elizabeth Russell.

Burn, Witch, Burn (also known as *Night of the Eagle*). Independent Artists. Director: Sidney Hayers. Released: 1961. 87 min. Black/white. Screenplay by Charles Beaumont. Stars: Peter Wyngarde, Janet Blair, Margaret Johnston, Anthony Nicholls, Colin Gordon, Kathleen Byron, Reginald Beckwith, Norman Bird, and Judith Scott.

Witches' Brew. Embassy Home Entertainment. Directors: Richard Shorr and Herbert L. Strock. Released: 1980. 99 min. Color. Screenplay by Syd Dutton and Richard Storr. Stars: Lana Turner, Richard Benjamin, Teri Garr, Kathryn Leigh Scott, Jordan Charney, and Kelly Jean Peters.

The Devil Rides Out (also Known as *The Devil's Bride*). Hammer. Director: Terence Fisher. Released: 1967. 95 min. Color. Screenplay by Richard Matheson. Stars: Christopher Lee, Charles Gray, Nike Arrighi, Leon Greene, Patrick Mower, Gwen Frangcon-Davies, Sarah Lawrence, and Paul Eddington.

The Exorcist. Hoya Productions; Warner Brothers. Director: William Friedkin. Released: 1973. 122 min. Color. Screenplay by William Peter Blatty. Stars: Ellen Burstyn, Max von Sydow, Lee J. Cobb, Jack MacGowran, Jason Miller, Kitty Winn, and Linda Blair.

"Mazes and Monsters." Made for television (Lorimar, dist.) Director: Steven H. Stern. Released: 1982. 100 min. Color. Screenplay by Tom Lazurs. Cast: Tom Hanks, Wendy Crewson, David Wallace, Chris Makepeace, Lloyd Bochner, Peter Donat, Anne Francis, Murray Hamilton, Vera Miles, Louise Sorel, and Susan Strasberg.

Rosemary's Baby. Paramount; William Castle Productions. Director: Roman Polanski. Released: 1968. 136 min. Color. Screenplay by Roman Polanski. Stars: Mia Farrow, John Cassevetes, Ruth Gordon, Sidney Blackmer, Maurice Evans, and Ralph Bellamy.

The Wicker Man. British Lion. Director: Robin Hardy. Released: 1973. 102 min. Color. Screenplay by Anthony Shaffer. Stars: Edward Woodward, Christopher Lee, Britt Ekland, Ingrid Pitt, Diane Cilento, Walter Carr, Lesley Mackkie, Lindsay Kemp, Irene Sunters, and Geraldine Cowper.

John Saul

Primary Sources

Brain Child. New York: Bantam, 1985.

Comes the Blind Fury. New York: Dell, 1980.

Creature. New York: Bantam Hardcover, 1989. New York: Bantam, 1970.

Cry for the Strangers. New York: Bantam, 1979.

The God Project. New York: Bantam Hardcover, 1982. New York: Bantam, 1983.

Hellfire. New York: Bantam, 1986.

Nathaniel. New York: Bantam, 1984.

Punish the Sinners. New York: Bantam, 1978.

Second Child. New York: Bantam Hardcover, 1990.
Suffer the Children. New York: Bantam, 1977.
The Unloved. New York: Bantam, 1988.
The Unwanted. New York: Bantam, 1987.
When the Wind Blows. New York: Dell, 1981.

Secondary Sources

Chambers, Andrea, and Joni H. Blackman. "Careful Plotting for Success Lets Thriller Writer John Saul Enjoy All the 'Creature' Comforts." *People,* 26 June 1989, 79.
Contemporary Authors. New Revised Series, vol. 16. Detroit: Gale Research, 1986, 343.
Kisner, James. "Interview: John Saul." *Mystery Scene* 16, 4.
Kramer, Laura. "John Saul: 'Remember, It's Only a Story.'" *Twilight Zone,* November 1981, 14.
Wiater, Stanley, "John Saul." In *Dark Dreamers: Conversations with the Masters of Horror,* 173. New York: Avon, 1990.

Filmography

"Cry for the Strangers." Made for television. Director: Peter Medak. Released: 1982. 100 min. Color. Screenplay by J. D. Feigelson. Cast: Patrick Duffy, Cindy Pickett, Lawrence Pressman, Claire Malis, Brian Keith, Robin Ignacio, Jeff Corey, and Taylor Lacher.

Splatterpunk

This section contains works that can be considered representative of the splatterpunk movement, although authors listed here should not be thought of exclusively as writers of splatterpunk.

Garton, Ray. *Crucifax Autumn.* Arlington Heights, Ill.: Dark Harvest, 1988. New York: Pocket Books, 1988 (titled *Crucifax*).
————. *Live Girls.* Shingletown, Calif.: Ziesing, 1990. (First published in a cut version by Pinnacle.)
Matheson, Richard Christian. *Scars.* New York: TOR, 1988.
Sammon, Paul M., ed. *Splatterpunks: Extreme Horror.* New York: St. Martin's Press, 1990.

Schow, David J. *The Kill Riff.* New York: TOR, 1988.
———. *Lost Angels* New York: Bantam, 1990.
Skipp, John, and Craig Spector. *The Cleanup.* New York: Bantam, 1987.
———. *The Light at the End.* New York: Bantam, 1986.

Chelsea Quinn Yarbro

Primary Works

Blood Games. New York: St. Martin's Press, 1979. New York: Signet, 1980.
A Candle for D'Artagnan. New York: TOR Hardback, 1989.
Crusader's Torch. New York: TOR Hardback, 1988. New York: TOR, 1989.
Dead & Buried. New York: Warner, 1980.
A Flame in Byzantium. New York: TOR Hardback, 1987. New York: TOR, 1988.
The Godforsaken. New York: Warner, 1983.
Hotel Transylvania. New York: St. Martin's Press, 1978. New York: TOR, 1988.
The Palace. New York: St. Martin's Press, 1978. New York: TOR, 1988.
Path of the Eclipse. New York: St. Martin's Press, 1981. New York: TOR, 1989.
The Saint-Germain Chronicles. New York: Timescape/Simon and Schuster, 1983.
Signs and Portents. Santa Cruz, Calif.: Dream/Press, 1984. New York: Jove, 1987.
Tempting Fate. New York: St. Martin's Press, 1982.

Filmography

Dead & Buried. A Ronald Shusett Production. Director: Gary Sherman. man. Released: 1980. 92 min. Color. Screenplay by Ronald Shusett and Dan O'Bannon, based on a story by Jeff Millar and Alex Stern. Stars: James Farentino, Melody Anderson and Jack Albertson.

Index

The Author

Cosette Kies has read horror and occult literature for a long time. She has reviewed horror literature for *Voice of Youth Advocates* for 10 years. In addition to writing numerous articles and books in the field of library science, she has authored *The Occult in the Western World: An Annotated Bibliography* (Hamden, Conn.: Shoestring, 1986) and *Supernatural Fiction for Teens: 500 Good Paperbacks to Read for Wonderment, Fear, and Fun* (Littleton, Colo.: Libraries Unlimited, 1987). She is currently chair and professor of the Department of Library and Information Studies at Northern Illinois University, DeKalb, Illinois.

The Editor

Patricia J. Campbell has taught adolescent literature at UCLA and is the former assistant coordinator of young adult services at the Los Angeles Public Library. From 1978 to 1988 she reviewed young adult books in a monthly column for the *Wilson Library Bulletin*, for which she now writes a monthly review column on the independent press. Her five books include *Presenting Robert Cormier*, the first volume in Twayne's Young Adult Author Series. In 1989 she received the American Library Association Grolier Award for distinguished achievement with young people and books. She and her husband, David Shore, write and publish books on overseas campervan travel.